The Learning Challenge

The Learning Challenge

Dealing with technology, innovation and change in learning and development

Nigel Paine

KoganPage

LONDON PHILADELPHIA NEW DELHI

Publisher's note

Every possible effort has been made to ensure that the information contained in this book is accurate at the time of going to press, and the publishers and author cannot accept responsibility for any errors or omissions, however caused. No responsibility for loss or damage occasioned to any person acting, or refraining from action, as a result of the material in this publication can be accepted by the editor, the publisher or the author.

First published in Great Britain and the United States in 2014 by Kogan Page Limited

2nd Floor, 45 Gee Street	1518 Walnut Street, Suite 1100	4737/23 Ansari Road
London EC1V 3RS	Philadelphia PA 19102	Daryaganj
United Kingdom	USA	New Delhi 110002
www.koganpage.com		India

© Nigel Paine, 2014

The right of Nigel Paine to be identified as the author of this work has been asserted by him in accordance with the Copyright, Designs and Patents Act 1988.

ISBN   978 0 7494 7125 5
E-ISBN   978 0 7494 7126 2

British Library Cataloguing-in-Publication Data

A CIP record for this book is available from the British Library.

Library of Congress Cataloging-in-Publication Data

Paine, Nigel, 1952-
   The learning challenge : dealing with technology, innovation and change in learning and development / Nigel Paine. – 1st Edition.
      pages cm
   ISBN 978-0-7494-7125-5 (paperback) – ISBN 978-0-7494-7126-2 ( )   1. Organizational learning.
2. Employees–Training of.   3. Organizational change. I. Title.
   HD58.82.P35 2014
   658.3'124–dc23

                                                                                           2014023527

Typeset by Graphicraft Limited, Hong Kong
Printed and bound by CPI Group (UK) Ltd, Croydon CR0 4YY

CONTENTS

ACKNOWLEDGEMENTS

There are many people who have helped in one way or another with this book. Their help, inspiration and dedication runs through the pages. I have an image in my head of the person I wrote this book for, but also very strong images of real people working in corporate learning all over the world and doing an excellent job quietly and thoroughly. They represent the future of corporate learning and I am deeply grateful for their inspiration and time. Those whom I interviewed I thank for the endless questions they answered, and their practice that they allowed me to observe.

Specifically I would like to thank some of those people individually: Ben Betts, Sam Burrough, Dr Celine Mullins, Stephanie Dedhar, Alison Shea, Stefanie Moring, Katharine Revel, Sharon Claffey Kallouby, Bob Mosher, Kenny McFee, Charles Jennings, Andrew Jacobs, Cheryle Walker, Dr Robert Demare, Dr J Keith Dunbar, Nick Shackleton-Jones, Julie Clow, Henry Stewart, Anne-Marie McEwan and Traci Fenton. I would also like to thank those who took the time and trouble to comment on first drafts of chapters, particularly Chapter 5 on impact measurement: Carol Stroud, Nicole Patterson, Blaine Rada, Jane Botsford, Ruth Haddon, Mike Buttery, Erna Alfred, Nic Laycock, Dr Wendy Green, Dr Urbain Bruyere and Diane Adams.

I took inspiration from the giants in the field like Elliott Maisie, Allison Rossset, Harold Jarche and Robert Brinkerhoff. Also my friendship with Donald Taylor, Sarah Carr, Con Soldatis, Linda English, Susan Metros, Stuart Rosenfeld, Wayne Hodgins, Bob Baker, Dr Doug Lynch, Martin Couzins and many more, has added considerable substance to this book. Of course, its weaknesses I own alone!

I also owe a debt of gratitude to the faculty and current and past students on the University of Pennsylvania CLO Doctoral Program. They really are stars in their own right. Particular thanks to Dr Annie McKee, the Program Director, for her guidance and trust. We have had many great conversations.

The editorial staff at Kogan Page have been unfailingly pleasant and helpful and given good advice. Thank you, Kasia Figiel, Liz Gooster, Katy Hamilton, Nancy Wallace and Anna Moss.

Finally, I would like to dedicate this book to the three women in my life. We are on a learning journey together, and together will take the hills and the rocks in our stride. Thank you Erina, Emily and Sophie for all you have said and the many things still left to say.

Introduction

I wish I could have read this book when I first began to run a large corporate learning department. It would have been so helpful to have been given a grasp of the overall scope of the role really fast and to have some of the immediate challenges illuminated. Ironically, this book, written for the most part in 2013, looks nothing like the book I would have read eight years previously. Fundamentals are pretty much the same but everything else has shifted dramatically: over half the chapters in this book would have been impossible to write eight years ago and virtually none could sit comfortably with that book from 2004. In some ways the enormity of those changes is another key reason why I felt that it was time to write this book and why I hope that a lot of people will find it not just helpful but essential reading.

There are many shelves of books on aspects of corporate learning but I could find nothing that tries to look across the piece and genuinely feed in information and ideas to flesh out what might be sketchy or illuminate what is unknown. If these books exist, they are well out of date. If you are new to corporate learning then this book will scope your job; if you are already there it will fill in gaps and challenge your thoughts and assumptions. Its modest ambition is to improve the quality, scope and ambition of corporate learning. And it can only do that by promising to:

- make claims that are evidence-based wherever possible;
- use case studies to illustrate abstract concepts or ideas;
- tap into a network of global learning leaders who helped scope the book and check it for accuracy.

This book should be like a personal coach. It will help you take the first steps towards embracing new ideas as well as deliver an in-depth analysis of specific topics. It will ask you questions and help you shape your ideas; each chapter will help you develop your own action plan that bridges the gap between theory and practice or from what should happen to what will happen. But you can also use the book for reference and, if you want to read it from cover to cover, as a continuous narrative. It just depends on what you need and when you need it. The premise is that this book will be useful, or rather essential. It has been written to be a core part of any learning leader's toolkit. You can let me know if I have succeeded.

In Chapter 1 we meet Katy on the first day in her new role as Head of Learning and Development. Her case is not atypical: there are many people like her, working on the best way to make the most of their role and have an impact on their organization. If Katy's story resonates with your position or describes in part how you feel, this book is very much for you. I know that if Katy had had this book at her side, she would have been able to work out her priorities, develop a strategy, and begin the process of building an L&D operation fit for purpose in the 21st century and fit for purpose in the organization she worked for. I hope you will find it equally useful.

I have divided the book into three parts. Part One sets out the challenges of work and learning, and is a manifesto of sorts for change in learning and the wider workplace. Part Two is rooted in the practical applications of learning in the workplace and covers key areas such as impact measurement and instructional design. Part Three looks at some huge seismic shifts that will impact directly on how we will think about and deliver learning in the workplace. You cannot be a competent and effective learning leader if you have not thought about how what is now known about the brain changes the way you organize learning, or how big data will impact on your analysis of need and monitoring your effectiveness. The technology context is critical now: no learning leader can delegate responsibility for embracing more and more technology in the delivery of learning.

This book can be of general interest to those working in the people sphere in organizations or who want to more clearly understand the imperative for lifelong learning at work. But for those deeply involved in learning at work, it will help you innovate, change direction and vastly improve what you do and how you do it, as well as how you measure your impact. None of this is just what I think: it is based on interviews and discussions with many people involved in learning and the people dimension at work. Many were learning leaders, but some were chief executives and directors of human resources. I owe them all a debt of gratitude for their honesty and frankness, and their input gives me some confidence to say what I have said.

PART ONE
The Manifesto for Change

The changing context for learning

Katy's story

Katy walked into the open plan area that she was going to call home. This was her first day as head of Learning and Development (L&D) and she was excited but slightly nervous. She lifted a hand, in a general way, towards the team and they responded enthusiastically. This was a team under pressure, and a team whose value had not always been appreciated by the rest of the organization; they were looking to the new leader to help. In fact, it was more than help – her task was etched in their faces: to save them from extinction!

Katy for her part was well aware of the problems, well aware of why she had been brought in, and she saw this as a tremendous challenge which, however exciting, was extremely daunting. Her mentor had been very encouraging; he had explained that if you took over a very successful operation it was really hard to make an impact and often all your efforts were concentrated on keeping the place at precisely where it had been before you took over. On the other hand, transforming a department in difficulty meant that you could really make a difference and that your contribution would be noticed. This was her first go at running an entire L&D operation. It looked like a mountain to climb on day one, but it also felt exhilarating. She took a deep breath before completing the journey to her desk.

She did not sit there for long. There were a number of key people in the organization who wanted early meetings, and she had been scheduled in to a series of 20-minute briefings with the senior executives of the company. She had hardly had a second to introduce herself to the team or work out who was who before she was whisked away to her first appointment and that, basically, was the morning gone. More meetings in the afternoon, and then finally, an opportunity to say hello to everyone in the team before she went home. She hoped every day was not going to be this kind of whirlwind and she would get the opportunity to actually do some work.

At home she gathered her thoughts. The team clearly was looking to her to defend their position within the organization. Executives saw her as the person who would trim, focus and develop the operation into something they wanted, and that could help them with the challenges the company faced. The messages were abundantly clear: the CEO wanted action, the CFO wanted cuts, and the director of operations wanted help. She had to deliver on all three but she had no idea where to start. Her head was flooded with ideas. She had options too numerous to count, and she had to work out where to start, what pace of change she could deliver, and what promises she could make that were challenging but realistic. She knew she had to create an entirely L&D operation that reflected more accurately what the organization needed, and help deliver its business objectives. There was less clarity, however, about where to start and her timescale for action.

Katy had clearly not been employed to shore up a failing department or defend everything it did, but neither did she want to close it down and start again. The challenge for her was to make it fit for purpose, and help deliver change. She wanted to support her people as they went through some fairly dramatic modification to their operation, but she also needed to understand the company and its challenges clearly and be seen as someone who was good news for the organization as a whole and gain trust and credibility inside the top team. This, she knew, was a delicate balancing act. As she fell asleep the first ideas for action were beginning to form in her mind.

There are many like Katy out there facing similar dilemmas because work is changing and the demands of work require a new relationship with learning. This chapter sets that process in context.

The changing workplace: who cares about an engaged workforce?

What makes some companies really great places to work? And what does it mean to work in a company or organization that feels like a learning organization as opposed to any other? The answer has got very little to do with salary or perks, or qualifications obtained. It is more the sense that you belong, that you are doing useful work that is recognized and acknowledged and that you operate in an environment that embraces new ideas, where there is widespread trust and respect amongst the staff at all levels. Learning is an integral part of great workplaces. And as our world changes, continuous learning becomes not a luxury for the few but a necessity for the many.

We have known for a long time, at least since Robert Levering's 1988 book, *A Great Place to Work: What makes some employers good – and most so bad*, that some employers are better than others; that some organizations encourage learning more comprehensively than others, and that some organizations are more productive and more successful than others. What we have become more aware of is that all these factors are linked.

There are indeed great employers who can turn demotivated, demoralized and switched-off staff into engaged, motivated and productive team members. However, the great place to work is pretty much the exception rather than the rule. Most workplaces are full of underused potential, unengaged and uninterested employees who care little for their customers and little for the complex processes of innovation, continuous improvement and personal development.

Both Henry Stewart in *The Happy Manifesto* (2011) and Gary Hamel in *The Future of Management* (2007) quote from a global survey which suggests that only 21 per cent of the workforce feels that they are fully engaged (Hamel, 2009). That leaves 79 per cent of wasted productivity, under-utilized human resources and general disillusionment. A huge Gallup survey in the United States in late 2013, called 'State of the American Workplace' reinforces this message. The Chairman's Introduction to the survey states:

> Of the approximately 100 million people in America who hold full-time jobs, 30 million (30 per cent) are engaged and inspired at work, so we can assume they have a great boss. At the other end of the spectrum are roughly 20 million (20 per cent) employees who are actively disengaged. These employees, who have bosses from hell that make them miserable, roam the halls spreading discontent. The other 50 million (50 per cent) American workers are not engaged. They're just kind of present, but not inspired by their work or their managers. (Gallup, 2013: 2)

Julie Clow captures this sentiment in her book, *The Work Revolution* (2012): 'employees have no sense of empowerment; they feel like victims in a gigantic, tragically unmovable system... Everyone gets trained... [but] absolutely nothing has changed'. This is a significant organizational deficit. Clow's solution is to start what she calls 'a work revolution' to do something about it. If we want to examine why learning has to change, she believes that we need to focus, initially, on why the workplace has to change, how work is changing and so how learning has to respond.

If we want some practical steps to change the workplace, we can turn to Stewart (2011), which lists 80 ideas for creating a happy workplace. These ideas are clustered around 10 core themes:

1 The imperative to trust your staff.

2 Making people feel good.

3 Openness and transparency.

4 Recruiting for attitude and training for skill.

5 Celebrating mistakes.

6 Creating mutual benefit.

7 Building a strong community.

8 Encouraging people to love work but also have some work–life balance.

9 Selecting managers because they are good at managing people rather than as an inexorable process of career development.

10 Encouraging staff to play to their strengths rather than forcing them to deal with their weaknesses or work in areas in which they are unsuited and therefore unhappy.

Clow has four points in her manifesto (2012: 17), which have parallels with Stewart's ideas. She believes:

1 It is possible to love your work, your workplace, and your work colleagues.

2 It is possible to find a dream job and excel at it, regardless of educational qualifications or job level.

3 Every organization can thrive, generate more value for its customers and shareholders and be more successful if it hires people who belong in that organization and they stick to the things they do best.

4 The workplace is not a zero-sum game where either the employees win or the organization wins. It is, in her view, in the best interests of employer and organization to build something in the best interests of the employee. That is what leads to a thriving profitable business.

Clow's thesis is that the problem of employee engagement needs to be addressed on a grand scale rather than one organization at a time. Her idea is to change the entire world of work: in other words, she would like a complete rethink about work everywhere. But in thinking big, her view is that we should keep it simple. The method of doing this is to make as many people as possible in an organization responsible for its achievements and outcomes. This includes leadership, the workforce and even customers.

This view aligns pretty closely with Clark (2012) in his book, *The Employee Engagement Mindset*. He believes that the single biggest obstacle to employee engagement is the employee. 'If you feel underused and undervalued, you can do something about it... Nobody can instil in you deep and rich and vibrant engagement. You have to do it' (p 6). Clark focuses on individual actions to develop engagement (intrinsic factors); Henry Stewart and Julie Clow focus more on the extrinsic factors (what an organization can do to encourage engagement). Both are critical. There is also a third factor that adds to the pressure to make big changes: the economic and social shifts that are turning our world upside down. In many ways this third factor is sweeping everything aside in its wake.

So we need to take a very broad view about how and why work is changing. These are neither cosmetic changes nor temporary changes in fashion but fundamental shifts in how we work, why we work and the nature of the work space. Technology is certainly a big part of this, but there is a more fundamental economic realignment occurring that underpins and stimulates these shifts. Guillen and Ontiveros (2012) call them 'global turning points' that present fundamental challenges for business. These include having to cope with increasing uncertainty and complexity in the external environment, dealing with a global economy that is out of balance, the increasing quest for sustainability at every level, coupled with a world of increasing inequality and the tensions that this engenders.

The 2013 Global Trends report (Strategy Dynamics, 2013) amplifies some of these points. It highlights the shift from abundance to scarcity of resources; the rapidly falling boundaries between companies and their communities; the shift towards distributed control and distributed power in the fight for value creation; and a range of new values and beliefs that this distributed world stimulates. The report highlights five imperatives for business, and the need to rethink:

1 the playing field in terms of competition;

2 your relationship with the consumer;

3 how you connect;

4 your agenda so that it is focusing on the future rather than protecting the past; and

5 your vision, values and role as a leader.

These are all massive challenges and as they impact, organizations must respond. This leads to fundamental shifts in not just what organizations do, but the way they do it. This requires a realigned workforce. So it is easy to see why the L&D operation inside any business is a significant asset in this process. If it fails to adjust, it will inevitably become irrelevant. If rightly aligned, however, it can address some of the people issues that will allow these shifts to take place quickly and smoothly. But this means that the L&D operation will also have to change radically in terms of its perspective and its focus.

CASE STUDY   Anne-Marie McEwan

Some of these necessary changes impinge upon the nature of the workplace environment. As the external environment changes, the workplace environment has to be rebuilt alongside the core of the organization. To understand that relationship more clearly, I spoke to the workplace environment expert, Anne-Marie McEwan.

She is strongly of the view that workplace learning cannot survive in isolation or as a 'nice to have' adjunct to the main day-to-day business. It is part of the hidden, as well as the tangible, physical and cultural make-up of the organization. This is one of the core ways that people's skills, values and behaviours impact on workplace performance. And if you want to make an impact on performance, you have to understand what drives an organization at the micro-logistical level as well as the macro-strategic level.

Her early realization that workplace and performance are inseparable, came when she and her colleagues at Cranfield University were asked to design a generic information system for the delivery of real-time operating information to the empowered teams on the shop floor, to enable and support continuous monitoring, adaptation and innovation. She believes that the learning operation should tap into the tacit knowledge from the shop floor and undertake, as a key part of its role, to make that process of knowledge exchange far more fluid and comprehensive. She believes passionately in the Japanese model that has, as a core belief, the idea that people on the shop floor are the source for solving workplace problems, and their involvement directly in that process should be a fundamental part of the way that work is organized.

She is convinced that it is possible, in manufacturing, to do things cheaply and to a very high standard. You can only do this if you tap into the knowledge of people at the sharp end of work and marry that with insights from customers. She can see no justification whatsoever for the separation of work from learning. Indeed, as organizations change, work becomes almost inseparable from learning and learning from work. When learning is separated from operations and put into HR, that barrier between learning and work defines and limits the effectiveness of the learning operation. She endorses the views of Hamel (2007) that the business of management needs to reinvent itself to best serve the needs of organizations in the 21st century, and part of that reinvention is to create a culture of continuous learning that has innovation and improvement at its heart. Learning, therefore, becomes an underpinning philosophy and an ever present process, rather than something that is done to you from time to time that gets in the way of work, and appears to be disconnected from it.

If you look at the nature of continuous improvement, it is about building up the collective intelligence and confidence of the shop floor and developing, in all staff, a critical eye that spots when things are not working, and they feel empowered to do something about putting it right. This is an alternative definition for learning that locks it in firmly with critical thinking. This is a philosophy and approach rather than 'a thing delivered'.

This process is not something that only applies to the manufacturing sector. McEwan believes it applies broadly across all work, in all sectors. And as work invokes this logic, it becomes more deeply embedded in the culture and values of the organization. As part of this mix, McEwan sees informal learning and social networking to be important methods for sharing that tacit knowledge she believes is so critical to an organization's success. But these processes have to be managed so that they are not misapplied or mangled in such a way as to act against the best interests of the organization. For example, if your model of organizational improvement and development only concerns cost-cutting, you will create a culture where there is no incentive to really share. Delivering change and making the argument for change should be closely linked to the process of delivering more innovation, creativity and excitement and making everything better, not worse.

The workplace and performance

The nature of the workplace impacts on performance, and the concept of the workplace embraces both the physical and the virtual. As people gravitate towards more flexible working, and the ubiquity of technology essentially allows work to take place almost anywhere, the nature of what constitutes the work space or the workplace is evolving fast.

There is a danger that the formal, physical place of work becomes the least attractive environment in which to work when compared with home, or even Starbucks! We should build much better environments at work and create virtual spaces that are functional and exciting to use wherever we happen to be located. The key to making all of the different working environments successful is the deployment of good communication technologies. There is an inherent contradiction between the need for tight communication security and the need for a flexible communications environment. Workplaces are grappling with this contradiction and attempting to resolve it, but the inexorable movement is towards enabling multiple spaces for multiple purposes that are all connected by a seamless technology web.

Anne-Marie McEwan has strong views on the design of work space. She cites a paper by the workplace ethnographer Judith Heerwagen on 'the psychosocial value of space'. Heerwagen (2008) determines the features of the workplace that need to be designed and built in order to be able to distribute and share our insights and feel comfortable in doing so. Her belief is that it is possible and hugely desirable to build workplaces that promote psychological and social wellbeing. Knowledge sharing and insight development as well as informal friendships are an extremely important element and a critical by-product of this. She uses a clear example from another world – the revolution in zoo design. Cages have now largely been replaced by spaces that make the animal feel comfortable and at home. Many workplaces, however, have not progressed beyond cages! She lists a number of wellbeing needs that should be met in contemporary workplace design:

- opportunity to engage in spontaneous social encounters;
- opportunity for relaxation and psychological restoration;
- opportunity for privacy and for movement between interaction and solitude, as desired;
- opportunity for learning and information sharing;
- opportunity for connection to the natural environment;
- opportunity for regular exercise;
- sound levels not much above or below that of nature;
- meaningful change and sensory variability;
- an interesting visual environment with aesthetic integrity;
- sense of social equity in respect;
- ability to maintain and control personal comfort;
- making sense of the environment.

If you add all of these together you see an environment that encourages thinking, reflection and sharing of knowledge and insights; you will not get this if the environment actively prevents it. That is why Heerwagen wants these processes embedded into the design of the workplace environment itself.

If you go into the office space of companies such as Google you can see her philosophy in action. The Google head office in London, for example, includes what is called 'the library' – a space for quiet reflection, writing and solitude which is in direct contrast to the generally febrile, animated environment of the main offices. And there are spaces for sharing ideas: small spaces for two or three people to meet and larger spaces for greater numbers, including whole-staff presentation areas. This allows staff to share their work in progress so that the company's output is part of a collective responsibility, which in turn yields widespread support but also (and very important) the enhancement of ideas because they belong to everyone. It should not matter where we are (either inside the physical space or connected online) when parking our thoughts and sharing them with others. Clearly the working environment should try to enhance this process. Unfortunately many actively inhibit it.

Technology and the workplace

More and more evident is the simple proposition that where you happen to be working should be your workplace. Technology should be embedded to the point where you feel part of that workplace and able to share your ideas with people there, regardless of where you happen to be. Frank Duffy, the architect, describes this as 'workplace 2.0'. He believes that all work-places are becoming distributed. We are almost returning to an earlier age: the diarist Samuel Pepys saw the whole of London as his office! Duffy (2008: 8) claims that:

> the unit of analysis is no longer the shorthand of office buildings and departmental boundaries – how anachronistic the term 'headquarters' already seems – but the sum total of all the many and varied spaces and places within which and between which highly mobile, electronically networked, knowledge workers are already operating successfully.

In other words 'work is what you do, not a place to go' (Duffy, 2008: 6). The physical office is a manifestation of the culture of work and this has to extend into multiple spaces. At the BBC media campus in White City, for example, the Starbucks cafe has the BBC IT network extended into it so that staff can work in the cafe and hold meetings, if they choose to. This cafe has been incorporated into the workplace but offers a radically different kind of environment to the main offices. The media campus has been designed to encourage staff to visit different buildings and each building has hot-desk spaces so out of town staff can plug in and work in any facility. The street furniture in the large courtyard has been designed to facilitate outdoor working during the summer. Instead of staff being locked into a cubicle or specific space for their working day, each department is encouraged to own and make use of the entire space. This encourages networking and cross-functional communication. Each area looks and feels different because it reflects the culture of each different function. What would otherwise be anonymous, identical floors have colour and character and some local ownership.

Google's workplace is designed to be attractive to its workforce. Engineers are encouraged to work in their offices rather than at home in order to spread ideas and build personal networks. This embraces the Japanese attitude to quality where working systems are owned widely and consensually and staff work together rather than being in a metaphorical boxing ring dancing around ideas and not engaging or cooperating.

This same idea has been picked up by the motor manufacturer BMW. Its R&D office has a transparent atrium where the different teams congregate so that work in progress is visible and R&D is literally connected. The need to develop and share knowledge is therefore both a metaphor and visible to all: the atrium works on both literal and symbolic levels. So, successful innovation has a definite relationship to the physical space and workplace culture.

The pharmaceutical company GSK's R&D centre failed partly because the professional culture among the scientists was not based on sharing and communication. As Sir Andrew Whitty, the CEO of GSK said: 'drug discovery happens in one brain, but drug development happens at scale and in a community' (2013). He talks about building 'an invention culture' to translate from mind to factory. This process of moving from one brain into the wider community is determined by the layout of the workplace, the structure of the workforce as well as the culture of sharing and relocation. To reinforce his own message with action, Whitty has set up open collaboration models in GSK allowing outsiders to win GSK support and resources to develop new drug ideas and build a wider community outside the walls of GSK to exploit innovation faster.

Many organizations are building diverse teams to run projects. To be successful, the teams have to adapt and learn to speak each other's language and listen to each other's views so that a multiplicity of ideas and opinions can be brought together. This is one way of solving increasingly large and complex problems at work. However, what are now well researched and proven insights, are not being manifested fast enough in the redesign of the workplace or the learning function. Both of these things should align. Every organization that wants to thrive needs to have processes and cultures that focus on sharing, refining and ultimately actioning ideas. In the words of Anne-Marie McEwan: 'the key is not to isolate knowledge from what needs to be done'.

Performance cultures

If you develop a performance culture with key performance indicators first, then put boundaries around them to focus on what can be delivered, but ensure that those boundaries are permeable and allow insights and ideas to be shared, then these separate components will join together so that each can add value to the whole. This is the approach used by Google and by GSK. It means that learning can be an embedded and integral part of the process and culture at work. It also allows a profusion of small, cheap prototypes to be tested and new ideas to be incubated in full view, not secreted in dark corners, so they get the widest attention and support before they are put out into the main arena or scaled up at cost.

It is clear that changes are happening in organizations, but only in pockets and in some industries. The speed of implementation depends on the nature of the competition and how entrenched existing cultures are. The more competition, the more willing companies are to try new methods in order to survive. And there is competition for the right staff in both recruitment and retention; this war for talent is increasing the speed of change. The simple fact remains that to get the best from your staff, they need a stimulating environment where they can work together and share ideas and make progress wherever they are located. A culture that enhances this process and accelerates the uptake and development is needed.

I asked Anne-Marie McEwan which industries, in her opinion, were furthest ahead. Her rule of thumb was the ones that need the most new ideas and innovative processes to survive are furthest ahead; these include the biotech, games, pharmaceutical and creative industries. She points to the West of Scotland as an area where the old industrial models collapsed in the mid-1970s and have been replaced quietly by new high-value biotech companies. The creative heritage of the traditional comic producer DC Thompson, based in Dundee, led directly to the key role played by the University of Dundee in helping set up games-developing software companies locally. This wave of the old being transformed into the new, as new skills and new knowledge develops new industries, needs to be accelerated in her view, for healthy renewal to take place.

The situation in Scotland is not all good news. If DC Thompson spawned a games industry in Dundee, the replacement of shipbuilding by giant call centres is not such a forward-looking step. Nor is the fact that universities, in general, are some of the biggest users of zero-hour contracts for support staff. A fundamental part of McEwan's philosophy is that you need to treat people well and design workplaces that enhance their feeling of wellbeing if you want to get the best from them. This is borne out by many other conversations I have had and by the research on workplace effectiveness.

On the whole, however, there are transformations that are taking this country forward, which are becoming more accepted and more prevalent without yet being dominant. What is clear is that everything discussed above implies a completely new configuration of the role of learning. Learning is at the heart of ideas, innovation, sharing and development. In this context, it looks very lonely locked away in the middle of the Human Resources department!

Change at work

The nature of work is in flux, which means that new models need to be tested and monitored for their effectiveness. This process, in turn, has changed and will continue to change the nature of learning at work. John Kotter, the Harvard professor and leading figure in change management, talked about 'organizational operating systems' (Kotter, 1996). The traditional hierarchical system of work organization, he felt, had enabled organizations to perform well in their current guise. However, to encourage innovation, continuous improvement and a regular exchange of ideas, a different kind of operating system was required. He chose to call this the 'network operating system' (Kotter, 2012). Every organization needed what he called 'a dual operating system' that was both hierarchical and networked. This meant that day-to-day processes were managed well in the orthodox operating system, while ideas and innovation was developed in parallel in the networked system. In this, connections were made not to roll out products and services but to accumulate possibilities and potential.

The simple concept he elaborated was that staff clustered to solve problems outside the normal structures and, once initiatives had been developed, the networked team disbanded and other groups formed. Kotter did not see these operating systems as mutually exclusive or dominating in organizations.

He felt that they had to run in parallel and staff, while working in the hierarchal system, would need temporary and voluntary network system roles. Organizations that wanted to facilitate increased innovation and smoother change processes would need to invest in building their network operating system while at the same time optimizing the hierarchal system to maintain day-to-day optimum efficiency.

CASE STUDY   Traci Fenton, WorldBlu

Traci Fenton is the founder and CEO of WorldBlu, a global community of individuals and organizations committed to embracing freedom rather than fear in the workplace. WorldBlu has been around for almost 20 years and about 250,000 people work in WorldBlu-certified organizations. Embedding democratic and freedom-centred structures in the workplace, WorldBlu believes, has a significant impact on innovation, performance, morale, motivation *and* the bottom line. The by-product is a more productive and happier workforce.

Traci Fenton's fundamental assumption is that the operating models in most organizations are incompatible with the age in which these organizations are now working. With increasing knowledge working, fear and command and control models are obsolete. She believes that toxic and horrible work environments will disappear in a process of almost natural selection because they have failed to evolve. Part of the reason for their demise will be that their best staff will want to work in a different kind of environment, so they will desert at the first opportunity. Workplace support and organizational success are indelibly linked. WorldBlu demands that the contribution of every single employee is recognized, and holds that the global epidemic of disengaged employees is morally disgraceful and massively holds back economic growth and development.

WorldBlu has now amassed a significant body of research that supports these theories that link happy organizations with increased productivity. (Henry Stewart of the Happy Company would say amen to this!) Why then, if this research is so conclusive, are organizations so slow to embrace the necessary change? Traci Fenton's belief is that the necessary shift is emotional, and a latent fear of the democratic workplace holds back managers from this kind of change. WorldBlu's proposition is that only a freedom-centred company can constantly and consistently innovate. In a fear-driven environment, staff become myopic and focus on not making mistakes and just doing their job. If we expect no more of them, they will do no more than the bare minimum to stay out of trouble.

These ideas are not new. Fenton highlights the former CEO of the furniture manufacture Herman Miller, Max Depree, as a model leader who developed a highly democratic and brilliantly innovative organization that was also highly profitable. She highly recommends his best-selling book, *Leadership is an Art,* which has sold over 800,000 copies.

Innovation

There are two kinds of innovation in organizations, according to Fenton. The first is what she calls 'messy innovation' where there is a confused pile of ideas and only one in a hundred has any chance of going forward. The second kind of innovation she calls 'inspired creativity' where the organization taps into the collective intelligence of its employees and customers on a continuous basis. It operates in a non-stop cycle, moving from assumption, through exploration, to action.

Working with complex processes is increasingly part of an organization's DNA. Fenton's description of 'inspired creativity' implies an innovation model where you move from convergent to divergent thinking before converging on an agreed action. This cycle of challenging naive assumptions and seeking out complexity builds resilience and problem-solving skills. This requires an organizational culture that encourages diverging thinking and deliberately enters what Kaner (1998) refers to as 'the groan zone' before the convergent phase offers resolution and a working solution. Great organizations manage to exploit the tensions and disagreements of the 'groan zone' to come to new insights and great ideas. Handled badly it is a recipe for dissent and tension, which is why trust has to be at the core of resilient and challenging workplaces.

At the heart of the freedom-centred company has to be organizational democracy and trust. This allows the building of energy throughout the organization, not just on the highly incentivized and motivated executive floor. This energy can only survive in a relaxed and stress-free environment. The archetypal democratic and freedom-centred company that WorldBlu cites is Zappos, the United States-based shoe seller (now owned by Amazon) that has widely shared its model of employee and customer engagement and building a 'fun' environment at work. When you go into companies like Zappos, you leave feeling energized and optimistic. This contrasts markedly with toxic companies. There, Traci Fenton is convinced, you always emerge drained and stressed.

Talking to customers

Customers are very demanding and can drop an organization or a service very quickly if it does not respond to their changing needs. If, however, we can engage with them and incorporate their help and ideas, the organization can move far faster than one that is locked into a reference system that does not include customers.

Zappos' tag line is: 'engage employees and wow customers', a philosophy that is now shared via workshops and boot camps that Zappos runs through a separate company called Zappos Insights. It clearly shows that an innovative culture is built on a supportive democratic workplace and an obsessive desire to talk to customers and incorporate their ideas. Zappos has been certified by WorldBlu as a freedom-centred company.

Where to start?

There is one key question that Traci Fenton asks executives in every company she visits and it will do well for us. It is: 'What would you do if you were not afraid?' This helps create a vision of how a particular company might look if it embraced organizational democracy. This helps in the introduction of the 10 principles for organizational democracy, which include open dialogue, listening, open book management and transparency about the numbers. These 10 principles are non-negotiable. Organizations work towards embracing all 10 or they cannot be accredited.

As the rest of this chapter has shown, an integral part of an effective organ-ization is that it embraces a strong corporate learning culture. A significant part of this culture is the ability and desire to move information around the organization fast, and create opportunities for staff to learn from one another. This begins to define the key facets of leadership. It is all about knowing how and when to use power; developing a compassionate and nurturing culture; and helping everyone connect so that they pull together and everyone feels they can give their best. The glue that cements these three areas is, of course, trust – a word that will crop up again and again in this book.

To deliver this, many organizations have to rebuild themselves. The qualities they need to engender are: trust, support and integrity through the organiza-tion, not compliance and control. This is a simple but effective checklist for everyone. Traci Fenton believes that insecure people create control structures, and that democratically-oriented leaders are humble and centred and don't feel the need for overt control. This requires organizations to develop, first and foremost, self-leadership on a grand scale. This is an organization where staff are willing to learn and work constantly on improving the organization by listening to its customers, and take responsibility for their own actions rather than blame others.

This idea has led to the establishment of the quadruple bottom line, a concept that Traci Fenton helped popularize. This reviews organizational performance from a financial perspective, but also in terms of an organization's contribution to the community and its internal and external environment. WorldBlu's philosophy can be summed up simply as: 'in a new age, we need a new model of business'. This chimes with the core philosophy of this book: in a new age, we need new models of learning. We discuss some of these approaches and models alongside the people that built them in the following chapters.

Work is changing

In his seminal book, *Intellectual Capital: The new wealth of organizations*, Thomas A Stewart wrote:

> Information and knowledge are the thermonuclear competitive weapons of our time. Knowledge is more valuable and more powerful than natural resources, big factories, or fat bankrolls. Wal-Mart, Microsoft, and Toyota didn't become great companies because they were richer than Sears, IBM, and General Motors – on the contrary. But they had something far more valuable than physical or financial assets. They had intellectual capital. (Stewart, 1996: *xi*)

Stewart defines intellectual capital as 'knowledge, information, intellectual property, experience – that can be put to use to create wealth'. He divides intellectual capital into three core categories: human, structural or organizational, and customer. What engendered this revolution in wealth creation is the emergence of the information age powered by microprocessors. If jet engines changed the economics of air travel, and plastic altered the manufacture of consumer goods, computers touch every industry and change the nature of work for almost everyone:

> not since Edison domesticated electricity has a technology revolutionized life the way this one has. It can prepare an invoice, animate a velociraptor, and sew a seam. The technology of information, a revolution in itself, is only a fraction of the larger revolution, of the Information Age. (Stewart, 1996: *xix*)

In a knowledge economy, it should (almost by definition) be very hard to separate learning from work. The core purpose of consultancy firms, for example, is to share knowledge internally to solve problems externally, and when they are global, they share knowledge rapidly around the world. This is because what works in New York may also be helpful in solving problems in Dubai or Mumbai. What those organizations sell is global insight matched with local knowledge.

Stewart's philosophy and understanding is echoed by the UK economist, Frances Cairncross in her book, *The Company of the Future* (2002). In it she defines the management challenges that the communications revolution poses for business. She lists 10 significant rules for survival. The very first is 'manage knowledge' because 'the company is the sum of what its people understand and know how to do well. Value lies increasingly in creative ideas and knowledge'. What she predicted 12 years ago has now come true.

It is clear that, to manage knowledge, intelligence, creativity and teamwork will be critical. The building of environments that sustain innovation, creativity and knowledge sharing should become a core facet of learning leadership in organizations. Given that managers will have to learn, as she says, 'new ways to explain and lead', how fast those new ways are developed and embedded becomes a make or break issue. Cairncross is attempting to address the human dimension of the corporate revolution, which has to embody a new and challenging role for learning and development. L&D will be at the heart of sustaining and creating great organizations and helping them address the issues of complexity that they confront every working day.

In her final chapter, Cairncross reminds us, that 'intelligent people are the most valuable resource of the company of the future' (2002: 188). We know that their attraction, retention and deployment are absolutely fundamental to thriving. To the three actions she lists, I would add a fourth task: development. The critical ability to learn and relearn will be a key way to develop and extent their intelligence. In a new organizational structure where 'old pyramids will go; new webs will replace them' (p 204), the individual will need to be empowered to take decisions, communicate and function autonomously within those networks, and share and acquire knowledge on that journey. This is not a model where learning is imposed or delivered in bits, but one where learning is constant and core. It is not one where learning occurs periodically at fixed points in fixed places, but one where learning happens everywhere all the time, and the responsibility for learning rests firmly with the individual. This is the only way companies will be able to acquire their 'more fluid shapes' as they 'form... and re-form, around talent and ideas'.

The workplace and the work space

The nature of work is changing fundamentally. In spite of claims by the new CEO of Yahoo! – Melissa Meyer – that working outside head office is detrimental to team spirit and creativity, increasing numbers of employees have no fixed working abode. They can hot desk in the office building, work from home or choose any number of other locations. Indeed, the UK temporary office accommodation company, Regus (**www.regus.com**) is rebranding itself as 'the third space'. The third space is neither home nor the office but somewhere in between. It is a local office shared by a range of companies and individuals, offering administrators support, work space and meeting space. The original idea of temporary office occupancy for a few months while a new company gets going, or a relocating company gets established, has become office occupancy for hours or at most days at a time, but the relationship is permanent. The major traffic is short term, and what is required is access to office facilities and a place to log on reliably to the corporate network. The key to belonging, or the definition of being at work, is logging on to the company network. Once you are connected, it is possible to work more or less anywhere for most of the time.

This shift in what we consider to be a place of work has enabled new organizations such as Central Working to flourish. Central Working offers flexible work and meeting space for a set monthly fee, which turns the semi-nomadic status of its members into an asset by encouraging the small companies who use its facilities to network with each other and cross-sell services. A small software company can trade with a small marketing company and a small website design company without ever having to leave their shared office space. This is knowledge and skill sharing in action. Far from seeing the lack of a dedicated office space as a temporary blip, Central Working is building a home base for a whole new generation of small knowledge-based companies. Even the physical layout looks different. People do not work independently at desks: they share workbenches and can retreat to individual carrels if they need to make phone calls or concentrate intently on a particular project. Membership of one site offers access to all sites wherever they are located in the country. Regus has exactly the same policy: a membership card gives you access to any Regus business base across Europe or the United States.

In a recent radio programme (BBC Radio 4 'News Quiz', May 2013), the panel had a discussion about the percentage of the working population that could go about their daily business while on a train journey. Provided the train had Wi-Fi, or a reasonable cellular connection, most members argued that a majority could continue their daily work with the advantage of having something interesting to look at out of the window if they got bored. Someone countered by suggesting that for a plasterer, a rail journey would not be a very effective way of continuing his or her business. This was immediately challenged by another participant. That person suggested that a rail journey could be the perfect place for a plasterer to catch up on invoicing and paperwork, or order materials online that could be delivered directly to the workplace, ready to start work, once the destination had been reached. And if the plasterer was really on the ball, he or she would have had the 'books' managed by someone in India or the Philippines, so the train journey would present the perfect opportunity to liaise, or take stock, or think about the future, or plan that perfect piece of plastering!

In reality, the corporate IT network has become more important than the building for work. At the BBC White City media campus, for example, staff simply went home when there was a major server failure. Even though they were in their office, virtually no work was possible without access to the network. For the BBC, countless other organizations, and even that plasterer, these are remarkable shifts in the concept of work. The time-limited, office-based 9-to-5 world is changing to a more flexible environment with accelerated delivery and increased velocity. We may not always be in the office, but we are 'always on'.

A senior civil servant once explained to me the convoluted journey high-level documents used to go on before they could be approved. The first draft would start life in a folder and be carried manually from building to building, department to department, office to office and desk to desk, in a slow linear progression. At each stop the document would be checked, commented upon and amended before moving on. 'Urgent' meant several days at the very least. When the document finally came back it was covered in alterations made by hand and initialled so it had to be retyped (possibly more than once) and then rechecked and approved. Now, in an age of e-mail, tracked changes and wiki-type documents, the same process can take less than an hour. And of course, physical proximity to the office building has nothing to do with that process. All that matters is physical proximity to a computer or even a smart phone that is logged onto the network.

The component parts of the workforce have also changed radically. Once, you were surrounded by people who were on permanent contracts the same as you. Now there is an array of permanent, temporary and free-lance staff, staff who work for suppliers, and outsourced staff who all share the same physical or online space and work together as a team and share the same goals.

The older models of learning, aimed at full-time permanent staff, will not wash in this new environment. That former exclusive target group for corporate learning seems as outdated as the 9-to-5 workday. Learning is caught up in the cauldron of change as much as any other part of the business. Therefore, the pace of delivery, the size of the components that are going to be delivered and the target audience for them need to be radically adjusted to remain relevant. Alongside this radical change in delivery is the need for entirely new skills, competencies and behaviours. For example, Procter and Gamble (**www.pg.com**) now claims that 50 per cent of new products are developed using crowdsourcing and open innovation. Even in more conventional product development processes, these new concepts play an increasing role.

So how do you prepare staff for these changes? What new skills will they need to make this way of working effective? Surely any useful learning leader will need to work with 'the crowd' outside the company, as well as the company staff on the inside? These big shifts will require major responses. And if this constitutes a 'modern' workplace, how will we know it is fit for purpose and successful?

What is work?

There are innumerable books on improving workplaces, and the link between a better work environment, increased productivity and greater innovation. Some of them focus on the role that the individual can play in building his or her own personal environment, others on how to develop better workplaces that create better work environments and increase productivity and effectiveness at work. One of the latter books, *Contented Cows Still Give Better Milk* (Catlette and Hadden, 2012) has a self-explanatory title and devises its approach and philosophy from a series of case studies of companies that have delivered a better workplace experience to their employees, and excelled as companies as a result.

An excellent book that focuses on the area of personal happiness is Rao's *Happiness at Work* (2010), which takes the reader on a personal journey. It focuses on what the individual can do to make his or her life – particularly work life – more meaningful, and encourages self-reflection, meditation and a focus on the positive:

> This book will show you how to bring joy back into your life. It will return you to the halcyon days of your youth when you thought McDonald's was a four-star restaurant, when you preferred nickels to dimes because they were bigger, and when snow was an amazing experience and not a bother to be shovelled away. (p 4)

It is about self-control, and control of self. Rao points out that you, as an individual, 'get to choose the emotional space you occupy. You can choose to be happy or miserable'.

Much of this 'self-help' and positive thinking emerged from the important research that began at the University of Pennsylvania and elsewhere, focused around the research of Martin Seligman, which became known as 'positive psychology' (Seligman, 1990). The articulation of Seligman's theories was developed further in his 2002 book, *Authentic Happiness*. Seligman and others in the positive psychology school had a dramatic impact on thinking and on clinical practice regarding, for example, depression, but also popularized the concept of personal empowerment at work and more widely.

Another key strand about the individual and the way he or she relates to the world emerged from the emotional intelligence research of the 1990s, popularized by Daniel Goleman's book, *Emotional Intelligence* (1995). This concept has its roots in the work of Thorndike in the 1920s and his concept of 'social intelligence'. Goleman and others took emotional intelligence much further by breaking it down into five separate components: self-awareness, managing emotions, motivating oneself, empathy and handling relationships. These qualities are, clearly, an important element in determining success at work and leadership competence. The research on which this is based looked at thousands of successful leaders and the skills and attributes they manifested. These ideas were extended into a workbook that encouraged intentional change under the banner of 'resonant leadership'. This was a practical repackaging of the early research work on emotional intelligence conducted by Goleman and colleagues, and resulted in a book: *Becoming a Resonant Leader* (McKee *et al*, 2008). The focus is still on the self, but mediated through the lens of work, and is firmly aimed at workplace effectiveness through self-knowledge and managed change to increase effectiveness and impact.

These themes also emerge through books that cover areas such as mindfulness and personal self-development. These bridge writing that is focused on business and an almost Buddhist focus on meditation, reflection and self-awareness. The workplace lens is there but in a far less focused way than in *Becoming a Resonant Leader*. The most well known of these books is by Google engineer, Chade-Meng Tan: *Search Inside Yourself*. This book emerged from a course developed and run by Meng inside Google that was aimed at Google staff, over 7,000 of whom have taken the course to date. The book led to the establishment of the Search Inside Yourself Foundation that spreads the message and practice of mindfulness more widely.

There are, therefore, two bifurcations: the first is between the role of the individual, set against the role of the individual at work and trying to influence others. The second concerns the difference between focus on self-discovery, and a focus on being more able to control the external environment. In one sense, research on what makes work environments productive coincided with research on how individuals can control their moods, be positive, and thereby take control of their own wellbeing. The coming together of these two strands has produced a rich and varied literature that stretches from academic research to pop psychology. There is therefore a critical link between, in the words of Catlette and Hadden (2012) – 'the very real, tangible benefits of treating people right in the workplace' – and clearly defining just what 'right' means alongside some personal responsibility for taking the time and effort to move the workplace in this direction.

I will now spend some time discussing *The Work Revolution: Freedom and excellence for all* (Clow, 2012). The book is built on the premise that all workplaces have to radically change. That analysis is very straightforward: it is built on five simple rules for companies:

1 they should focus on impact rather than activities;

2 they should care more about energy than schedules;

3 they should focus on developing their employees' strengths rather than worry about job slots;

4 they should do the right things, but not everything;

5 they should build on the ideas and perceptions of the grassroots rather than only offer a top-down approach.

The focus on the individual is about being a player and taking responsibility for his or her actions; the focus on the leader is about building a team of engaged and excited employees; and the focus on organizational design is to build organizations that tend to encourage the right behaviour by employees and leaders.

Clow begins to touch on happiness at work: 'When individuals are tapping into the deepest potential and doing work that is meaningful to them, they will see their work, and the challenges at hand, as fun' (2012: 32). For Clow, work should be more like play for it to be more productive and for the work-force to offer up discretionary effort over and above those things demanded of them within their job descriptions. It is the duty of those who can influence the 'design, culture, or operations of an organization,' to make the 'fundamental changes... in policies, processes, strategies, and culture, to create a better environment' (p 33). The reason that all of this is so important is that work is changing dramatically, becoming more and more complex, ambiguous and uncertain and therefore the full presence of employees is required just for survival.

Work never stops, information never stops and companies are increasingly global and working with multiple cultures across many time zones. This imposes tremendous constraints but is also fantastically liberating in terms of how you manage your own personal workload and the autonomy you are granted.

All of this means that the 'old rules' that traditionally governed workplaces are increasingly irrelevant and new rules apply:

- Rule 1: *Impact not activities* – focusing on results and creating a strong performance culture, ignoring those processes or actions that are irrelevant or only loosely connected with performance at work.

- Rule 2: *Energy not schedules* – enabling individuals to expend the least amount of energy for the greatest effect. This means ignoring conventional time patterns of work and allowing individuals to define how, where and at what time they want to perform.

- Rule 3: *Strengths not job slots* – the hiring of people who fit your culture rather than fit your job description. Once you have the right people, it is possible to build the job around them all, and empower the individual to find the right role in the right team. It is about getting the right people to hire those new people who fit in with existing staff and whom you can trust from the very beginning.

- Rule 4: *The right things not everything* – prioritize: get staff to focus on what is important and what makes a difference.
  If everything is a priority, nothing is.

- Rule 5: *Grassroots, not top-down* – empowering individuals to contribute solutions to business problems and get them to work.
  It is about moving towards organizational goals by encouragement and open dialogue, not by bullying and sanctions. You cannot build rules to create this kind of environment: you need to take rules away and substitute trust and effective working.

What the *Work Revolution* is positing is a more democratic, empowered and trusting workplace in which the right people can flourish with the minimum of rules and regulations, operating with the maximum scope for building their own teams, taking decisions and doing the right thing for which they are appropriately rewarded. This means loosening 'our death grip on control' so as to unleash potential (Clow, 2012: 35).

It is an essentially optimistic philosophy that argues that by granting employees real freedom and autonomy it is possible, at the same time, to make them responsible for their results. It is possible to get a win/win situation in that the harder they work and the more seriously they take their role the better they will serve their customers. Clow uses Google as a case study that proves her points. Her conclusions marry together workplace organization, mindfulness and self-knowledge. Her final mantra is that:

- Everybody should know what they're working towards and play a unique and distinct role in making that happen.

- People should learn to respond to their natural rhythms, so we remain healthy and strong and push hard to get the job done.

- Healthy individuals mean healthy organizations. Strong organizational performance needs strong staff.

- These organizations know the difference between what matters and what doesn't, and staff are empowered to challenge each other to work this out.

- Any sense of urgency is based on real deadlines rather than arbitrary project plans. Something is done when it really needs to be done.

- Individuals are rewarded depending on what they bring to the organization, and organizations are successful when they reward those verifiable contributions (Clow, 2012).

There is more real evidence to suggest that workplaces which are happy and invest in staff are more productive than those that do not. One of the clearest indicators is given by the London Business School economist Alex Edmans, who researched the stock market performance of a number of companies that had a reputation for investing in their staff, against the mean overall performance over the same period (Edmans, 2011).

He used as his guide the list of the 100 best US companies to work for, which is compiled each year. Edmans tracked the companies in the list from 1984 until 2009 and found that these companies improve their performance by an average of 3.5 per cent per year, which was 2.1 per cent above industry benchmarks. In other words, these were good companies to work for *and* good companies to invest in. He makes three definitive conclusions:

First, consistent with human capital-centred theories of the firm, employee satisfaction is positively correlated with shareholder returns and need not represent managerial slack. Second, the stock market does not fully value intangibles, even when independently verified by a highly public survey on large firms. Third, certain socially responsible investing screens may improve investment returns. (Edmans, 2011: 1)

This is a remarkable paper, showing that theories on human capital investment prove that investing in people is inexorably linked to success, and this is validated in economic terms. By implication he undermines a whole sway of theories that see people investment as a cost to be minimized. He does this by a detailed analysis of performance over 25 years, and concludes that employee engagement and satisfaction positively correlate to shareholder return. This is not an assumption that is common amongst investment analysts even if it is a deeply held view amongst HR specialists, learning leaders and enlightened CEOs!

Edmans' main data source, the '100 Best Companies to Work for in America'. It has been published annually since 1984, and since 1998 has been showcased in the January edition of *Fortune* magazine. The companies that apply to be considered as great places to work are scored in four areas: credibility (communication to employees), respect (opportunities and benefits), fairness (compensation, diversity), and pride/camaraderie (teamwork, philanthropy, celebrations). Much of the score is based on detailed employee questionnaires, the rest on research into the companies. This process is both robust and respected. Being placed on the list improves recruitment, and there is intense competition to be listed. In spite of this data, it is generally ignored when investment decisions are made. Employee satisfaction 'is not directly capitalized, [it] only affects the stock price when it subsequently manifests in tangible outcomes that are valued by the market' (Edmans, 2011: 18).

What are the implications for the leader of learning?

The growing body of work that explores organizational health, individual wellbeing and workplace performance appears to be coming to three definitive conclusions. First is that there is a good economic case to be made for investment in people development. This is not just about wellbeing or functional competence for the organization, but a major step to excellence and high performance. The second is that learning cannot, should not and does not operate in isolation. Learning is only one component (however significant) of a high-performing workplace. Thirdly, there is evidence that it is possible to build a virtuous circle in an organization. This means that good employee engagement leads to higher organizational performance and increasingly shared knowledge and expertise that creates better engagement and better performance (see Figure 2.1).

FIGURE 2.1 The spiral of improvement, based on an original concept by Chris Yapp

Personal
learning =
hard and soft
skills growth

= Higher
performance

Increased performance
increased innovation
in the organization

Organizational learning =
shared knowledge and
cultural cohesion

The evidence that is beginning to emerge is highly significant and validates reasonable investment in learning but only where the learning function is fully integrated into the spectrum known increasingly as 'talent'. In other words, learning is part of a retention, induction and development strategy that aligns with broad-based organizational performance criteria. In isolation the data is not nearly so clear.

What emerges, then, are 10 critical tasks for the learning leader to revitalize the learning function and build a case for investment:

1 Learning leaders should align with any strategy in the company to become a 'best employer'. Even if there is no overt strategy in place it is really useful to assemble the data used by the US organization Great Place to Work and by the UK *Sunday Times* in its best employer list. Other countries may well have similar organizations and similar competitions but for data gathering rigour alone these two are worth examining in their own right.

2 Some of the criteria, eg linking development opportunities to performance, pride and celebration can be implemented formally or informally. The key is to see development as one of a collection of initiatives that lead to increased performance, not something stand-alone.

3 Impact measures of learning should take account of the broader picture and the total portfolio of opportunities. In many ways this

logic runs counter to the Jack Phillips ROI movement that attempts to isolate the impact of learning.[1] The research would seem to indicate that integrating learning into other employee development opportunities, and into the performance management systems, will ultimately yield better results.

4 The learning opportunity should be balanced with opportunities to apply the learning immediately in the workplace. The bottom line should be behaviour change, not competency acquisition. This requires discussion, integration and commitment, particularly with line managers and operational heads.

5 Stretch assignments should be a regular part of employee development that can be linked to, but not necessarily part of, formal learning. There is a key role for the learning team to intervene to ensure that this informal learning is reinforced and that any gaps in the learning are filled.

6 The learning strategy should be part of a much broader attempt to share knowledge across the organization and bring in knowledge and ideas from outside. This model goes beyond simple team development and becomes a far-reaching extension of workplace culture. This is worth fighting for as it will integrate into the broader learning strategy and therefore have a great impact on the ultimate performance of the organization. Modern business requires far more than great teams to succeed. Team culture is very well entrenched in organizations but the concept of sharing knowledge horizontally through communities of practice (first developed by Etienne Wenger in the 1990s) needs to be supplemented by an encouragement to develop external networks. If teamwork is indisputably effective in organizations, validated communities of practice are still very difficult to justify and developing external links and networks harder still. This requires a significant culture change to be effective. As an example, the formation of two companies out of the US Defense services company SAIC was a massive change initiative, but business as usual continued as two companies were created out of the single entity. One of the ways that this process was made easier was by putting in a social network across the organization so that staff could share issues, share knowledge and resolve problems without the constant intervention of HR executives. (Information based on an interview with J Keith Dunbar, VP Talent, Leidos; see Chapter 3.)

7 There is no compelling reason for the learning operation to remain within HR; it could equally well be part of operations and located within the business. There is also no reason for learning to be centralized as long as there are core functions and a common strategy.

8 The learning function has to get deeply involved in the business strategy. Its core purpose should be to help deliver that strategy. To be successful it should talk the language of business, win over key personnel in the organization and be at the heart of the business.

9 Learning has to be about developing, extending or maintaining the culture of the organization. This has to be explicit in everything it does and may well dictate how learning is managed. In other words, any content or subject matter that has to be delivered is an opportunity to reinforce or extend the organizational culture. It should certainly not run counter to it.

10 If we take Kotter's (1996: 183) five leadership competences that he deems essential to survive in uncertain and complex times, they form a template for how we organize formal learning programmes and how they are integrated with informal learning:

- Risk-taking: getting out of your comfort zone.
- Humble self-reflection: honest assessment of success and failure.
- Solicitation of opinions: aggressive collection of opinions and ideas.
- Careful listening: propensity to listen to others.
- Openness to new ideas: open-mindedness.

Learning that does not challenge and attempt to get learners out of their comfort zone, that does not engender ideas or help learners gather new ideas and create opportunities for self-reflection, may deliver the explicit content but will not deliver the implicit message on the profound new kind of leadership authority that is required. On the other hand, learning that attempts to build in these new competences has the advantage of developing explicit skills alongside implicit values. The Kotter list is not the only list, but it illustrates very clearly the direction of travel that is required to run organizations in this century.

FIGURE 2.2   Based on a conversation and original idea by Harold
Jarche (see **www.jarche.com**)

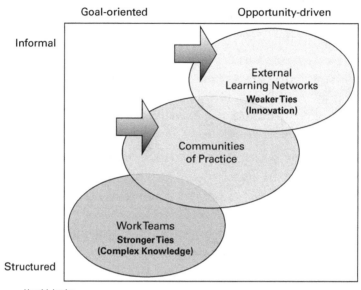

Harold Jarche

Conclusions

The management of workforce training dates back to the early part of the 20th century; we are now on the brink of something quite new. In essence, in much the same way as the internet changed our world, the logic of the internet will change our organizations, work structures and work practices. Hamel and Breen (2007) claim that management 2.0 'is going to look a lot like web 2.0', ie the defining characteristics of the web such as widely distributed creative tools, cheap and easy experimentation, power granted from below, voluntary commitment, fluid authority and natural hierarchies, are necessary to make 21st century companies operate successfully in their environment.

What is clear is that the role of L&D is central to the correct functioning of modern business. This is very good news for the learning leader. The corollary is that this performance will be indelibly linked to overall business performance, and nothing else will really count.

Note

1 Jack Phillips established the evaluation method based on ROI (return on investment). His work is developed and sustained through the Jack Phillips ROI Institute.

The learning leader role is changing

This book has been built on one very large assumption: that what is going on in corporate learning at this time is markedly different from what has gone on previously. The skills, competences and behaviours that marked out the successful learning leader in 2000 are, quite simply, inadequate in 2014. That does not mean that these changes have occurred universally and ubiquitously. The picture out there in companies large and small, government departments, not for profits and other organizations is very uneven. It is still possible, without looking very far, to find learning operations entirely focused on courses and course catalogues; evaluating success using 'happy sheets'[1] and having no input whatsoever into the strategic direction of the company.

I will argue and try to demonstrate that we are moving away from the traditional model that has held sway for 50 or more years, and that the trajectory is abundantly clear even if uptake is uneven. This trajectory takes us on a journey from an isolated self-contained quasi-autonomous learning operation to one that is fully engaged in and aligned with the business. It takes us from a course-catalogue approach to the rich provisioning of complex and multi-faceted learning environments. This moves us from isolated incidents of learning to a focus on continuous learning; from an obsession with formal, structured class-based learning to a balance between what is formal, experiential and on-the-job. We move from large, extended chunks of learning, delivered infrequently, to small focused granules often delivered at the precise moment of need. We shift from isolation to incorporation, and from management indifference and polite tolerance to enthusiastic embrace. Learning is neither arbitrary nor irrelevant but a critical core component of contemporary business success. This is quite a journey.

Our new learning leaders make a genuine difference to the organizations they work for, and they can explain that difference in tangible business terms. It is not about what people enjoy; it is about what transforms the efficiency and the effectiveness of their working lives. This is not simply the slow, inexorable path of technology push, but a revolution in the way work is organized and delivered, coupled with the committed and engaged response to these changes from the learning leadership.

This is so important that there really is no alternative scenario for corporate learning teams, apart from extinction. If the learning team will not engage with this new reality, evidence suggests that the organization will simply disengage from the learning team. In a world where it is possible to outsource large elements of learning creation, design and delivery, support and assessment, it is vital that the in-house team makes a tangible and demonstrable difference! I have talked to large numbers of learning leaders and actively worked with well over 100 in the last few years, and I am increasingly struck by the similar traits exhibited by those who are successful now and who clearly will be in the future. The benchmarks are rapidly being established. This does not mean, however, that successful learning leaders are clones of each other: precisely the opposite is the case. Learning leaders are people who have engaged with the organization they work in, and therefore gone down different paths depending on the learning needs and the business demands they have encountered. There are, however, similarities and obsessions that link them and offer a perspective and guidance for anybody in this field wanting to learn about learning.

My focus in this chapter could have been on any number of chief learning officers or their equivalent. I have chosen to work with a group who span Australia, Brazil, the United Kingdom, the United States and mainland Europe. They work in large or medium-sized companies as well as the public services. Their organizations have little in common, but the approach, philosophy and commitment they demonstrate in their work unites them on many levels. They are exceptional, but they are also truly normative. They have grasped the essence of the role in a way that is impactful and memorable. They are also open and articulate about what they have done and why, and what they wish they had done. They are clear about what they have achieved, but also clear about what has yet to be accomplished.

I conducted interviews with five learning leaders over a period of months. I asked them all similar questions and wrote small profiles of each person. What struck me forcibly was that, in spite of being in separate countries and working for very different organizations, much more linked those CLOs (chief learning officers) in attitude, spirit and achievement, than divided them.

In essence, there were 10 characteristics that set them apart from their colleagues. These people are the path-finders because they, and their employers, are ahead of the game. It is pretty self-evident that where these CLOs step today, the vast majority of learning leaders will have to step tomorrow. They offer cogent hints at a future that is, in some measure, scary and daunting but also hugely exciting and engaged. Those characteristics are:

1 Focused, above all, on business impact and willing to be judged on the effectiveness of that impact.

2 In spite of working with budget and staff constraints, they continue to deliver.

3 Always aware of what is going on in the 'third horizon' (two to three years out) for business and learning, therefore continuously revising learning strategies to realign with business strategy and available technologies.

4 Being generally very optimistic about the future and the future of learning.

5 Delivering astonishing results that are acknowledged at the very highest level of their organizations. Because they deliver, they have influence.

6 Having a technology focus rather than a technology fear.

7 Willing to cull outmoded programmes to incorporate new programmes and new ideas.

8 Building strong teams and strong networks.

9 Wanting to learn and encouraging others to learn by establishing coaching and mentoring cultures.

10 More interested in building environments and the resources to populate them than in building courses.

From the interviews, some common conclusions and behaviours emerged:

- Build a personal network of people who can share, help and offer advice when you need it. They will inspire you, guide and keep you grounded. Make a continuous effort to keep in touch and maintain the network. You will know very quickly who is worth developing that kind of relationship with. Share your successes but above all admit your challenges and the things that did not go brilliantly.

- Use action learning[2] as a way of embedding the change you are trying to sustain; ie organize peer groups to solve their own problems and support each other through the developments you are trying to initiate.

- Be an excellent facilitator. All the interviewees are good at facilitation, which includes exceptional listening skills. They are good at building groups who can facilitate and they develop facilitation as a core leadership skill in their organization.

- This group are innovators. It is innovation that solves problems and takes the business forward; it helps achieve the big business targets and is not innovation for its own sake.

- Alignment with the objectives of the business is almost so obvious it need not be stated. This group are great learning leaders but what they achieve is for their business. Their thinking and approach are totally aligned with what their organization needs to accomplish.

- They all run a variety of learning programmes, but they focus on the most important developments for the business rather than random offerings. A business has a handful of core objectives; an aligned L&D operation has a similar and related programme of activity.

- Good learning leaders know how to cull. They have to get rid of the less than critical in order to concentrate on what is most important and focus resources accordingly.

- Good learning leaders are in the culture change or the culture sustaining business. They know that they cannot do their job if the culture of the organization is not aligned with its objectives. They want to develop people and in a way that promotes a certain view of the world and a certain value system. You cannot do one in isolation from the other.

- None of the people I interviewed had a single solution to every problem and they never entered into conversations with the end in mind. They all had the ability to say 'no' and to see when a checklist, for example, would be more helpful than a learning programme. Their approaches were multi-faceted: online, informal, face-to-face or formal. It was all about what worked best in specific circumstances.

- They all made a point of proactively finding out about the business they were in. They made contacts, they visited different parts of the organization and they tried to understand what drives their business, or in the words of one interviewee, finding out: 'what keeps the CEO awake at night'. This was not a one-off initiative but a constant process of sustaining engagement.

Five learning leader case studies

CASE STUDY   L&D Manager, Local Government, London

This manager has been in post for five years and his role has evolved over that time from managing programmes to working out the strategic learning needs of the Authority. In other words the role has evolved from one of tactical management role to strategic leadership. His earlier team of six has now become a team of two (which includes himself) and he reports to the Organisational Development Manager who gives that team freedom to do what is needed across the organization. If he had to sum up the essence of the role, it would be: 'making stuff happen'.

The Local Authority has shifted as well. It now has a matrix-like structure that includes a dotted-line relationship between this manager and the subject matter experts in specific departmental areas like housing, children and social services. This fits in with the shift from an essentially transactional focus to a more strategic one; the transactional elements that were part of his role are now run in the appropriate business units. This is a more fitting home as it keeps the day-to-day operation of courses close to the people who make use of them, which helps ensure their validity. This, in turn, clears the way for the manager to work on future-facing strategic competency development. The range of compliance and tactical programmes are managed and run by the subject matter experts. He can offer advice and support to make those initiatives work well. For example, he can help develop materials, or improve them, but the delivery and responsibility for the subsequent programmes lies outside his direct remit. Others drive each programme and push it into its specific community and make it work. At a time of acute change, this frees up the manager to build the next generation of programmes and help keep the Authority fit for purpose.

He established a self-enrolling digital learning environment that now consistently achieves 1,000 enrolments per month – although this number is reducing as knowledge across the organization increases. It is a considerable uptake as the Local Authority has a staff of 3,000. This is a remarkable achievement and shows learning percolating into the heart of work, rather than being a one-off or something special. He is also encouraging managers to be active participants in their teams' learning.

His employer makes an average spend on L&D of around 2.5 per cent of total salary cost. He equates this investment with minutes of learning rather than abstract costs of learning. The 2.5 per cent total equates to an average of 52 minutes of learning per week per employee, and he therefore develops materials that fit into the 52-minute timeframe or multiples or fractions thereof; ie learning events can take 26, 13 or 104 minutes. A member of staff might spend 26 minutes, for example, looking at a case study or 13 minutes in a telephone-mentoring conversation. Sometimes, they can spend more time working on resources or materials if the need arises. The overall philosophy is to develop an environment where continuous learning takes place in very small bites every day or every week.

He is a great believer in Brinkerhoff's success case methodology (see Chapter 5) for developing his evaluation framework. This focuses entirely on the impact of training on the organization and gathering data that will measure that impact. He is not so much interested in the numbers going through, or enjoyment of the process! Essentially the model involves measuring the current state of affairs and then how much things have changed as a result of any kind of sustained L&D initiative. The movement between these two measurements can be roughly equated to the impact of L&D in a particular situation. In spite of the obvious benefits of impact measurement, he is still finding it difficult to convince some of the Authority leadership team that data focusing on numbers of participants and their degree of enjoyment of the programme rated against the four Kirkpatrick levels is neither required nor relevant (again, see Chapter 5). Old habits die hard!

His employer is in a state of flux at the moment as it is seriously exploring the possibility of radically changing its service delivery by managing services that are bought in for the community. This will require more than new skills for employees: it will require a complete change of mindset. He relishes this and other challenges that the role currently offers and his focus is on a radical reprogramming of capability and culture right across the organization. This is a far cry from managing a portfolio of standard, repetitive, skill and competency programmes.

He keeps in touch with what is going on by constantly liaising with the business units in the Authority. Although he is formally part of HR, he spends most of his time working with the business units learning about what they require now and in the immediate future. This is not simply absorbing information: he spends time horizon-scanning so that he can engage in discussions about his conclusions and how far they coincide with the perceptions of the service leaders. What emerges from these conversations is a series of scenarios that lock in with the various business units. These include what they think they will need in terms of human capability, what they think will happen to the organization over time, and what preparation they can make to ensure the right outcomes in terms of the success of the Authority. For this process to work, he has to make a sustained effort to speak their language and focus on the things they worry about rather than the things that interest him. His success will be predicated on meeting business challenges and focusing on agreed outcomes. He can see little value in gathering data on either throughputs or outputs when only outcomes really matter to the service leaders.

This Authority is a significant employer (it has, for example, the same turnover as the Next clothing group, although turnover is significantly reducing as budgets decrease). It is therefore not an easy ship to turn, and that is the challenge. His aim is to get L&D firmly into the Authority's workflow. With the staffing based more and more inside the business units, he wants his team to become the critical friends of those who are trying to run the various services the Authority offers. This is a leading, facilitating and influencing role, not a directing, managing or ordering one. He is also very happy to leave learning inside the business units and let it be owned and managed by those teams. He can help others do some of the more difficult learning design work and support the roll-out of new programmes, but leave the ownership local.

He stopped delivering an induction programme for new managers because the real value of intervention occurs only when a person has taken on the role and encountered challenges. If you are smart enough to get a manager's job the chances are, he believes, you are smart enough to start doing the job. Later intervention is, therefore, much more practical, productive and insightful. When new managers have begun working in their new roles they can begin to sense their own skill deficits or those of others around them. At this point they are most receptive to learning and much of the learning needs to be one-to-one, in a quasi-coaching format. So he has a heavy coaching workload himself, using colleagues to work with others. The next stage is to encourage his managers to work together, and to form action learning groups or self-study groups to work on their common challenges.

He is also passionate about the idea of leaders as teachers. There is now a vast array of experience in the Authority that could and should be tapped into by more junior leaders. These processes ensure that knowledge is shared and best practice built upon. That process also creates autonomous leaders who are capable of self-development and not reliant on others to do things for them. It is also true that examples from within the work community have much greater impact, and tend to be taken much more seriously than examples from outside, or theoretical models and abstract applications.

In essence, he is striving to build a learning organization, not a learning department. He is more inclined to develop sources and resources than courses. This forces learners to make sense of the material and build upon it and add comments or additional material. Around 30 per cent of content is now sourced from outside the L&D team and his target is to raise this to over 70 per cent within the next year.

Clearly then, he is an enthusiast for the 70:20:10 model (see Chapter 4). He accepts that the percentage break points between formal, informal and on-the-job learning are far less important than the focus on a holistic approach to learning. This is one of his core beliefs. To further that, he believes that building up a personal learning network as quickly as possible allows a learning leader to maintain a permanent perspective on where innovation lies and who is really pushing the boundaries. This, he feels, is better than concentrating on what is current good practice. Used inappropriately, this can actually kill off innovation and bring everyone's aspirations down to what everyone else is doing. He would always prefer to break new ground, solve new problems, in new ways, and generally radicalize the whole scope and practice of L&D so as to move learning into the heart of the organization.

He sees the support and encouragement of innovation as critical. This is because learning practice needs to evolve fast and become more flexible and efficient so it can meet the changing needs of his employer. Clearly there now has to be a technology focus but he feels it is wrong to get fixated on technology as a process. The issue is to use it as fully as possible during learning because it adds flexibility and velocity to the delivery. And he sees how important it is for his team to model the use of technology, and encourage people to do the same.

Other things, however, are equally important. For example, he has built local physical spaces where people can meet and debate issues that mirror the virtual learning environment on the intranet. His approach is always holistic and deliberately combines different modes of learning; for him, this is the only possible way forward: to open out learning and build learning into the heart of work.

Conclusions

The manager believes that what is now required in many organizations is a change in mindset. This is a massively important and complex process that involves the entire staff. Get this right, and behaviour can change rapidly. Mindset precedes behaviour change, not the other way round. One of the key ways to do that is to role-model the behaviour change that is being sought. But progress is sometimes frustrating, and he believes that local government needs to become more agile, and large numbers need to be involved in promoting and developing this. It is not the role of L&D but the role of L&D in partnership with key managers: it is the latter element that makes the difference. This means that L&D is at the heart of change, and without the active participation of L&D it is very difficult to see how sustained change will happen.

He is not interested in building learnt helplessness in his organization. What he is trying to do is quite the opposite: he is trying to encourage empowerment through learning. He wants everybody to feel that they can develop their own competences and not be afraid of the future. This is an enduring and significant aim for L&D. He puts this rather neatly when he says: 'You are either at the table, or on the menu.' That applies to whole organizations, and it includes L&D.

CASE STUDY Cheryle Walker, Former Head of Digital Learning, National Australia Bank

---

Cheryle Walker was until recently head of digital learning at National Australia Bank. NAB is Australia's largest bank with 28,000 employees and close to 1,000 branches. Her role is situated within the NAB Academy, which was established a few years ago as part of a significant employee value proposition on personal development and growth. The main Academy is in the bank's Docklands office; there is another in the Bourke Street, Melbourne head office, and smaller Academies in all the main offices in Australia's other state and territory capitals.

The Academy is a significant investment in people development, and creates a deliberate and focused showcase for groups and teams to learn and share. The space is also available for small meetings and quiet, individual reflection. Its location on the reception level in the Docklands office means that it is outside the security zone, and visitors can meet there without recourse to visitor passes or being signed in and out of the building. That makes the Academy a deliberately defined space outside the mainstream of the business with a different pace and a different feel. One of the themed workspaces has a stage and a costume area for role-play and other uses, and each room has a wall of garage-type doors that can be rolled up to bring the smaller space into the larger communal area.

It has video conferencing facilities and lots of technology but the Academy is largely focused on delivering face-to-face programmes. There is, however, a fast growing need for dedicated digital learning programmes. Providing these was, in essence, Cheryle's role. She argued for an extension of the Academy remit into asynchronous and synchronous digital learning, and worked on her own initiative to prove the case. Such was her success that she built up a team of nine to extend and develop the online learning portfolio.

The team runs a series of WebEx seminars, and has trained a significant group of staff from the bank's various businesses to produce, facilitate and run these sessions. Cheryle deliberately set out to destroy the prejudice that many staff had about webinars. She blew apart the initial perception that they were boring and simply vehicles for the passive consumption of someone else's PowerPoint slides, by insisting that her offerings would be structured around learner interaction every two minutes, and would involve breakout rooms for more detailed discussion of the topics being covered. She also made use of the company's IP telephony for the audio delivery so that any staff in poor online connection locations would not be disadvantaged. This sophisticated audio management system can handle audio break-outs to mirror what has been created in the online space. In essence she absorbed the spirit of the Academy's face-to-face output, and made online learning as equally productive and engaging as the mainstream offerings.

In addition to the webinar programme, her team built two new digital learning portals. One offers resources for self-learning via an iteration of the company's Sharepoint site. This initiative is based on the concept of portal-based learning, where the learner has complete choice of resources and pathways through the learning programme. The second is a YouTube-type channel containing video material that is managed by Cheryle's team but wholly operated day-to-day by staff elsewhere in the company. Anyone can upload anything relevant and then promote that resource internally by publishing and promoting the link. One of the more popular uses is to upload recorded meetings and post self-generated videos from within the business. Traffic to this site is considerable and the most popular and relevant resources have been downloaded and viewed thousands of times.

The three channels have shown a 65 per cent growth in usage during the year and represent part of a wider company culture change where a conscious effort is being made to develop a new digital awareness and a digital culture. The bank's social media hub located within the Academy in Docklands is an example of this. The team not only track all Twitter and Facebook comments about the bank and its affiliates and notify key staff accordingly but also act as an internship centre where staff can come and learn about social media and take that knowledge back to their own department and extend their direct use of it to gather information and to market their brand.

The key areas that Cheryle is focusing on include peer-to-peer learning, support and knowledge sharing: part of her remit included running online mentoring throughout the company. Her task is more and more about customer engagement and working out the right data points that will enable her to gather the right conclusions about what impacts most effectively on the business she works in. Her view is that this data reveals individual staff needs, as well as broad company direction. Her philosophy is therefore about meeting the needs and aspirations of individuals wherever they work in the company, and making a defined and measured contribution to the company's overall corporate objectives.

Conclusions

Cheryle Walker's rapid progress in four years at NAB is a clear indicator that there is room for the entrepreneur within a corporate structure. Cheryle tapped into what the organization needed, almost before it knew it itself, built a role for herself and then developed a team to extend capability and reach. Her approach is aligned with the broader online philosophy of the bank, so she is in line with current thinking, but at the same time changing the way the organization views learning. She also instituted permanent change in the process.

CASE STUDY   Dr Robert Demare, Deutsche Post DHL[2]

Robert Demare is the global head of learning and development for IT services, a captive internal IT provider for Deutsche Post DHL (DPDHL) and is based in Prague, in one of their global operation centres. He has been in this role since 2008. The role began as head of the training operation in support of the 3,000 IT staff employed by DPDHL. The role focused mainly on meeting all the IT services' technical training needs. The next stage of the evolution of the role came when Robert took on responsibility for leadership development. Now, some six years on, the role encompasses everything from induction, through technology training to engagement and change management.

As is a characteristic of many organizations, the scope of the role has grown substantially while headcount has decreased. However, there has been a sustained increase in impact as measured in the annual staff survey. This is not simply due to the current financial climate; it is a general characteristic of his domain. The role and focus are changing fundamentally and the old models (including staffing models) are being replaced by a realigned and reconstituted operation. Learning reflects and tracks the changes going on in the wider company.

To accommodate these changes, Robert has consistently framed the role differently from the one he inherited when he joined the company. He has shifted from only dealing with tactical issues to embracing a broad, strategic approach. He has encouraged the shift of much of the more rudimentary learning and development tasks into the operational part of the company. As resources become scarcer, Robert has innovated in order to maintain and indeed increase his impact.

The simple trend over the last five years has been that DPDHL's hard investment in training dollars per head has dropped by 24 per cent in the past four. But when employees in the company are asked, their clear perception is that the opportunities provided by the organization for development have consistently increased. The favourable response towards learning has gone from 64 per cent approval to over 80 per cent during those five years. This is a substantial achievement and part of the bigger debate about size of investment vs degree of impact. For DPDHL IT services employees, learning is much more about getting the right experiences than participating in training courses.

In the area of leadership development, for example, many of those involved in the delivery are drawn from the business itself and the small, core L&D team focuses on offering a consultancy and facilitation service, which allows the team maximum leverage and the greatest impact for the least possible cost. One of the big successes of this model has been their 'Active Leadership' programme, which acts as a community-of-practice for the 300 people managers within the IT division. The team's role is to facilitate discussion around topics selected by the small groups that takes this process forward. Most of the client group prefer to work in this way rather than to sit through formal courses. The sessions are geared towards an action learning[3] approach by focusing on the core issues that the managers face inside the company, which they select for discussion.

This process encourages the leadership teams to become more actively involved in improving the system that they work in, and the L&D staff facilitate this process and offer resources that can help. Outside these sessions, further development is offered through deliberately structured challenges and stretch assignments. This is clearly not a model of passive consumption of instruction: it is an enabling process that allows the organization to do something for itself and to be in charge of its own learning destiny. This process has been enthusiastically supported by the IT group's managing director who is aware of the power of informal learning, coupled with stretch assignments. He is keen that his leadership teams actively engage in reflecting on work processes to make them better, and to make the company more efficient and effective.

The key enabler for Demare has been to chop some of the lower-level tactical tasks such as managing compliance programmes away from his core role, in order to spend more time on strategy and work with and for the business roadmap. To this end, technical training is prioritized based on the most important business objectives ultimately driven by customer need.

Robert makes more time for networking in the organization and conducts regular sense-checks around his own plans with senior business stakeholders. The best piece of advice he received when he joined the company was that he would get a lot from finding out what kept the CEO awake at night, and then organizing his work around those issues. At this moment his core focus is on improving IT project management and driving change by increasing staff core skills as the business rapidly evolves.

The first task in achieving this requires a careful focus on what works and which staff have real expertise in delivering key projects on time and to customer expectations. Once he has that group, he can roll out their expertise, with some consistency, across the whole organization. Robert has to ensure that the right skills are in place to deliver this, and the learning emerging from the process as it moves forward is shared and defined.

The second task involves a radical rethink of how courses work and what alternatives there are to fixed-point programmes in favour of continuous learning opportunities. As time goes on, Robert thinks that many of the formal courses he is currently responsible for will get pushed away into the organization, to be managed locally or user-managed using technology. In any case, areas like technical up-skilling are changing so rapidly that it is impossible for a team at the centre to keep ahead of the needs of the staff at the sharp end. The engineers are clearly better at managing (and delivering) that for themselves. Right now 30 per cent of the DPDHL's technical up-skilling is delivered by internal people – and Demare expects this to grow over time.

Robert Demare is sure that on-demand performance support will become the norm, and be based around video-driven, micro-context support that the end-user can control. This will be offered in such a way that each individual can map what is available and work out what, and how much, suits his or her immediate learning need. Robert will therefore continue to expand his role of facilitation and community-of-practice building role, as this empowers key staff to get more interested in not just their personal learning but also the capability of their teams.

There are three key geographical centres where the vast majority of IT staff are based. Each has completely different age profiles and therefore learning needs and approaches to learning. The first is in Germany where the average age is highest; the second is in Malaysia where the age profile is far younger and many staff are under 30, and the third group is in Prague where Robert himself is based. Here the age profile slots somewhere between the other two: the average person is in his or her mid-30s. This means that a similar problem can demand different solutions from different centres. If one group wants a formal course, another will ask for access to YouTube to solve exactly the same problem. He has no issue with this. Part of Robert's role is to bring the entire cohort towards the same skill level at the same time. He also needs to move forward in such a way that the development of the whole IT operation is not held back by the slower adopters.

The 'Active Leadership' programme is liked because it brings staff together to focus on the challenges that they select for themselves; nothing is imposed. This model can be applied to other areas of L&D. DPDHL has embraced a management approach through its First Choice Way programme. Teams regularly meet around white boards to talk about problems, root causes, and ensure that continuous improvement is a part of daily life. This process takes learning out of a classroom and into day-to-day routine. If this is tracked against performance metrics, it will be a conscious and deliberate way of helping teams manage their development and monitor the resulting impact on the organization. The sum total of these will register the impact of L&D overall.

As measuring impact is increasingly critical, one key task is the focus on gathering the data that can define the impact of the programmes he is responsible for. This data is both quantitative and qualitative. One powerful source of data is gathered from senior leaders and managers across the organization when they share their perceptions of what has been achieved by the participants in a specific programme and what further needs to be done to improve effectiveness and efficiency. He initiates and sustains this dialogue.

To be able to maintain conversations across the whole organization, Robert has worked assiduously to build a personal network. He believes that relationship power within an organization can deliver more than status, or the power attached to a particular role, because relationship power is much more broadly based and impacts across the whole company. If you put yourself on an expert or status pedestal you are more likely to be challenged. If you build your credibility from the ground up it is more impactful and sustainable. His actual role is located within the HR executive, but he is often felt to be an integral member of the operational IT team.

Demare is clear that the perception of L&D throughout the rest of the organization is critically important. It is far better to create the right impression than it is to be forced to justify and defend your position all the time.

Innovation is a real driver throughout DPDHL, but it is innovation focused on business performance. This means that Demare's discussions around innovation are with key staff in the business. He is, therefore, not afraid to ask the right questions at the right time to broaden his understanding of core IT issues and processes so he can work out what is needed. The richer his understanding, the richer those key conversations. It would be almost impossible for him to do this role if he were not enthusiastic about the business as a whole, and knew who to talk to in order to get good advice and work out the practicalities of a project or learning initiative. This process is central to his work practice.

Demare also sees a key part of the role of L&D is to be the organization's storyteller, narrating the successes and sharing the achievements around the company in a way that resonates and sticks and can be learnt from. He believes that stories are important as they help communicate not just the facts but the underlying values and emotions around those facts, so that they are remembered. Clearly the internal communication department has to be involved as a partner in trying to do this, but he owns a core part of the narrative when the stories concern innovation and learning.

Conclusions

Robert Demare's career trajectory has meant replacing virtually all the tactical programmes he was responsible for with a more coherent and strategic role across the IT business. Where he can get out of the way and let the workforce self-select appropriate learning, he has done this. Where programmes belong more appropriately in the business, he has pushed the responsibility to the relevant operational unit. All the while he has kept an eye on the larger, emerging requirements of the company as a whole, and made sure that he understands what makes various elements tick and what his strategic focus should be.

Robert Demare is aware that he has a significant role in an organization that is growing fast and changing rapidly. To maintain credibility and extend his impact he has to move in an increasingly strategic way through the organization. What really matters is that what he offers aligns perfectly with the changing demands of the business. Nothing could be more important.

CASE STUDY   Dr J Keith Dunbar, Director Talent Management, Leidos

Keith Dunbar joined SAIC two years ago as the Head of Learning and Talent Development. However, both the organization and the role have evolved significantly during that period. The organization has now split into two, and Keith is the Director for Talent Management across the whole of Leidos. Leidos constitutes the more entrepreneurial part of the previous company. It has been rebuilt out of the old company to better ready it for the current more competitive climate and make it fit for purpose. It is therefore incumbent on Dunbar to create a new function that is equally fit for purpose. To do this, he has had to make significant changes in the way that L&D is organized and delivered and integrate it into the wider talent management framework.

The new role is a senior one covering the whole of talent management and development. Why the shift? Quite simply, he believes that the greatest impact occurs when there is an alignment across all the components of the talent management cycle. For example, previous leadership development programmes were poorly attended although the content was extremely important. The reason was that leaders were not rewarded for how well they managed their people or developed talent: during the performance management cycle only the financial metrics that they controlled dictated bonuses or promotion. Without aligning development, reward and performance management, it is impossible – or at least very difficult – for development initiatives to have the traction required to actually change behaviour and make a significant impact.

To Dunbar, this is a fundamental issue: the impact of the CLO working alone will always be diminished unless he or she has some control and influence over the way other aspects of the employee lifecycle are organized, valued and managed. This has other ramifications within the broader HR framework. In other words, L&D requires the right culture and context to sustain any kind of significant impact.

In Leidos, these ramifications mean that the traditional HR generalists, with their transactional rather than strategic outlook, have to be retrained to be able to take on more strategic roles in managing that same talent management cycle. From disconnected lower level operations such as managing compensation and bonuses, the same staff have now been given broader roles that encompass a more strategic overview of the needs of the company. The focus is on developing those aspects of talent management that can help the business to grow. The new HR is involved in business development and takes an active part in supporting and extending those areas of development that drive growth.

One of Dunbar's huge strides forward in building his new role was the establishment of a Talent Council run by senior business leaders in the organization. The Council's role is to help define and endorse strategic needs and point towards critical areas for talent development inside the company. That enabled Dunbar to focus his role, legitimately, on what strategic development was needed within each of those agreed segments. One of the key outcomes from that process was the identification of a clear need for an entirely new role within the company, that of Solutions Architect. A group with the potential to take on that new role was identified within the talent review process. The members of this group had their development needs analysed on an individual basis. They are now being established as a driving force within the company, and are being allocated roles in appropriate parts of the business.

It was evident from these high-level discussions that what had been lacking in the past had been cross-enterprise roles; the Solution Architects will fulfil that role and will develop into a cohort of key enablers with the ability to leverage technology and use a new and complex skill set to develop these new roles across the entire organization. These individuals in their new roles will make a disproportionate impact as they will pull the technology, skills and expertise from across the whole company into projects and activities. The decision to proceed with this emerged out of an integrated process of strategic analysis and holistic thinking. In other words, the new role is completely aligned with the aspirations of the new company and it needed someone in Dunbar's position to deliver it.

Previously, talent management and L&D were completely separate functions. Now there is one vice-president in the corporate structure and one person at director level with one team to support all the processes involved. Therefore, in spite of overall staffing numbers declining, the impact is considerably greater. The team is now focused on what is critical and strategic rather than routine and tactical. This means that managers are being asked to do more than they used to do, as well as increase their customer-facing role. Essentially, this translates into shifting the balance of ownership from a central team to the line and the business.

The three company values of 'Inspired to make a difference, Passionate about customer success and United as a team' now drive the heart of the development process. The new, leaner team will operate in a new way within the business. More responsibility has to be passed down to individual members of staff; for example they have to be trusted that they will sign onto programmes, get their credit and be able to self-certify. It is neither possible nor desirable to hand-hold staff during these basic administrative processes. In the same way, L&D can no longer monitor compliance training: it is pushed back to the departments to undertake. The managers in these departments are charged with overseeing the whole process. Accountability has shifted to those with a vested interest in success.

The Talent Council was the first indicator of what future governance for L&D might look like. Its focus was on alignment and its scope became the new HR business model. Its impact meant that senior leaders began seeing talent development as critical to the future success of the company. Alongside this came the definition of leadership behaviours and the establishment of a Jive[4] business collaboration tool to encourage sharing and begin a new form of informal and conversational leadership development. The Jive platform is now adding around 200 people per week who self-sign onto the platform. The leadership programme may use the MOOC[5] concept as a delivery model in the near future.

The process of building new leadership capability began with the definition of business requirements. These helped define some key strategic tasks and the key aspects of leadership behaviour that would be focused upon so that the tasks could be successfully completed. To make this a meaningful process, performance management had to be aligned so that the right leadership behaviour was incentivized. All of this was agreed before any programmes were instituted.

A new Leading@Leidos community was identified to smart push leadership and management content, and this will be the way that the Leadership MOOC will be built. Performance management competence and effectively managing talent have also been built into the core skills of leadership for the first time. Everything articulates with everything else.

The group also rebuilt the on-boarding programme. The initial programme was cut to two hours, but then participants were offered six months of additional support and acculturation, and continuing development through the Succeeding@Leidos community. This phase of the on-boarding process has been recreated on Jive to allow more extensive percolation through the company by self-selected mentoring opportunities.

Innovation and experimentation will be critical going forward. Over the next few years it is unlikely that the talent management function will absorb the compensation or talent acquisition functions, but the balance between buying in and building from within will significantly shift, as the value of development is proved in terms of speed and cost-efficiency. Along with this shift will be a transformation of the way the organization operates. There will be far fewer people managing internal poor performance, poor leadership and leadership violations, and far more focused on delivering business value. Around this will be a new culture of internal cooperation and team working across organizational boundaries as the Solution Architects role begins to bite deep into the organizational culture.

Conclusions

The underlying philosophy that drives Keith Dunbar and the way that he has developed his role has become the generic underpinning for L&D success. This philosophy is made up of four components:

1 Understand the business. Know why and how it is successful and what benefits it provides to its customers so you can see how your interventions can help. You need to be able to clearly articulate the value that improved talent management can contribute to the overall success of the company.

2 Always begin new processes or programmes by starting small, thinking big and scaling fast.

3 Try to make innovation the heart of your role, and imbue that philosophy across the whole team. This means not simply reading about other corporate learning initiatives but understanding the big changes in business and how L&D initiatives can provide increasing value to the organization.

4 Think holistically: a key part of the role is to work out how processes can be tied together differently for increased efficiency and effectiveness.

The drivers that will be the key to success in this role are almost entirely business drivers. Dunbar's focus is on building a more effective business through developing more effective staff. To do this, he has pushed the routine and day-to-day elements of his role out to the business units to manage, so that he can focus on what is critical and strategic.

It may seem axiomatic that a new company, with new challenges, should wish to rethink the contribution that a coordinated talent management function can deliver. But this role had to be built and argued for using clear business logic, and its success will be largely determined by the overall success of the new venture. There is no greater challenge for L&D than this, but no greater justification for investing in this function.

CASE STUDY Nick Shackleton-Jones, Director of Online and Informal Learning, BP

Nick Shackleton-Jones' view of learning's role is strikingly clear: it is to help BP staff perform, develop and connect. And he is there to support and guide his team in fulfilling that role. In other words, they will prosper if BP prospers. However, he believes that in order to fulfil that role BP has to rethink what corporate learning means and how it is delivered.

In his view, the only option is to place BP at the forefront of L&D innovation, or to fail to deliver through lock-stepping with the slow pace of change within the corporate learning industry. The need for change, and the traditional slow response to that need, has encouraged Nick to establish himself as a thinker and exponent of new approaches to corporate learning. In making a difference for BP, which is obviously the key driver, his team also hope to make a difference to the broader learning industry. He wants his operation to be seen as a pioneer and an innovator.

The need for change emerges from the fact that much of corporate learning is out of alignment with the businesses within which it operates. It has not kept pace with the way that much of current work practice has evolved and continues to evolve; it lacks solid theoretical underpinnings and ignores current learning research. Conventional corporate learning delivery borrows heavily from educational traditions dating back to an early industrial era, and is increasingly out of step with the ways in which people work and need to learn today. That conventional and still widely applied learning model is predominantly passive and academic – at a time when we know that engagement and practice-based peer interaction lead to more impact and sustained behaviour change. Furthermore, there is an increasing need for just-in-time activity, based predominantly on referencing rather than rote learning: just enough learning at the point of need.

If corporate learning is to deliver on the expectations of a workforce caught up in uncertainty and complexity, the learning processes have to be flexible and agile. It is all about building the kind of learning environment that creates opportunities for staff to learn continuously from each other, from critical incidents they confront, from peers and mentors, as well as from formal learning opportunities open to them. It is impossible to build this kind of model by simply pushing large chunks of learning out to specific target groups at set times. Work is no longer like that, BP is no longer like that and learning therefore has to evolve.

Nick Shackleton-Jones divides learning into two major areas that he believes should never be confused. The first is where learners already care deeply about something. It is where they have encountered a challenge and, in response, you have to satisfy the hunger of learners who can 'pull' the relevant information or resources and solve their own problems. The second is where learners are not (yet) concerned about something; in this instance the learning team have to supply both the relevant information and the affective context: in other words deliver motivation as well as content. Potential learners need to know how to engage at the moments when it is most valuable for them to engage. This can involve both informal and formal processes and sometimes they blur into one another.

Nick Shackleton-Jones is responsible for building his own team, and he increasingly hires people on the basis of the projects they have completed rather than the qualifications they possess. By doing this he can get those with real passion for a role, together with demonstrable capability. On appointment, the development of confidence, skills and attitude are managed by placing that individual within a supportive peer group. As a manager, he is able to judge the effectiveness of the group by the body of work they complete. It is about the tasks that have to be completed, and making sure that people can deliver those tasks efficiently and effectively; in other words, it is only about performance.

More and more of Nick's role is based on helping people connect performance with development. Learning may be just one of a number of ways in which the team can help staff perform, develop and connect. These days, the team spends more time developing resources and applications aimed at addressing the challenges staff face than constructing courseware. It follows, therefore, that one of the key ways you can find out if you have succeeded in this process is through an ongoing dialogue with the groups you are aiming to help and the people who manage them.

Other important metrics include gathering information on employee engagement, time to competence, and staff retention in the business. Key stakeholders will also tell you if your intervention in the process has helped improve those metrics or not. If you really want to evaluate impact, the best approach is a matched pairs experimental design. In this model, some go through the programme and some do not. The challenge faced by the learning industry is not the difficulty in measuring impact, but confusion over how to deliver it. Shackleton-Jones believes that the current ways we assess learning are ripe for deconstruction and innovation!

There is no substitute, in Shackleton-Jones' mind, for getting close to the problem and trying to understand it in context. His team has now reached a point where, when they ask, 'How can we help?', they know that they are asking a complex question. They see their intervention as part of a process for resolving the issue, rather than simply applying a predetermined solution or offering a pre-existing course or programme. The conventional content-oriented discussion is being replaced with a solution-oriented one. To give an example, there may be occasions when the creation of a simple checklist does more to impact performance than a complex course. You discover that only by asking the right questions, not by turning up with a solution in mind.

His team have developed a series of penetrating questions that cut through to the nub of the issue and involve the target audience in that enquiry. Some examples are: 'What have you done that really works?' and, 'How can we build on that, extend it, and deploy it more widely?' or, 'Who are the people who know what to do?', 'Is it possible to put more people in touch with the experts as mentors?' These are more productive and lead to more interesting conversations than simply offering a menu of programmes to choose from. The stark difference in roles is similar to the difference between a chef and a waiter. One creates; the other simply takes orders.

Corporate learning will evolve fast or fade into the background. Shackleton-Jones believes that if the learning function cannot or will not build appropriate challenges for staff out of which they can learn and apply that learning immediately in the workplace, the future is bleak. In that case learning retreats into compliance delivery to meet legal requirements and little else. The learning function remains tactical, administrative in outlook, and competent but uninspiring.

The alternative is a vibrant learning operation that focuses on building learning resources and applications. These are designed to challenge or support staff at the critical points in their career, such as on joining, promotion, taking a leadership role, running a large project, or changing jobs within the organization. In this model, the emphasis is on supporting staff at those times when they are keen if not desperate to learn. The outmoded alternative is to force-feed content at times when staff have no need or are resistant.

The new kind of learning team within an organization does not need to have a predominantly learning background. Rather, they need to understand the performance context so that they can engage in the right conversations and ask the right questions. Their target groups need to be centre stage since they may already be engaged in a collective effort to achieve the desired outcomes, and will best understand the conflicting pressures that have given rise to the current situation.

In turn, the team can build solutions targeted at meeting the desired outcomes and also take account of the performance context.

Innovation is therefore at the heart of Shackleton-Jones' core strategy. It is vital to innovate in order to move learning forward from something akin to alchemy to something more akin to chemistry. In short, having a good theory of learning enables his team to sidestep the quicksand of learning convention.

At the BETT conference in London in January 2013, Nick delivered his philosophy of corporate learning. Much to the surprise and amusement of the audience he delivered it in verse and from memory! The crux of his argument centred on two key roles for learning, which he defined as curation and creation. He means a curation that helps spread the stories of achievement and success, which can sustain key professionals at the top of their game. The measure of effectiveness is taken from the user not the provider. The second key role is creation, and not just of material that is 'so so' but is well designed and appropriate for the target group. That is what has impact. And what links those two approaches is the need to know your audience, in his words, 'through and through'. If you can deliver what your target audience cares most about, they will learn. And care and concern emerge irreducibly from knowing that audience really well and being able to speak their language and articulate their concerns.

Conclusions

Nick Shackleton-Jones has engaged with BP at a time of rapid change, and radically shifted the thrust of the role from catalogues of established programmes to smaller and more flexible resources. He has moved the emphasis from formal, slow development to informal and rapid solutions that are well designed and completely centred on the target audiences they are aimed at. He has taken on the big challenges of a very large company and has systematically rebuilt learning to fit the new circumstances and the new needs.

The key issues that emerge are:

- Learning provision cannot exist without context. It should never be just a course.

- The aim is to create independent learners capable of solving their own learning problems when they need to, not forcing learners into a set timetable that suits the economies of scale of the providers rather than the immediate needs of the learners.

- Learning has a huge potential role in helping the culture and values of an organization move forward.

- There should be no artificial boundaries between formal and informal learning.

- Performance support, ie learning or resources at the moment of need, is a crucial element of learning provision.

- You need to approach a problem with no firm solution in mind; if you do not you are in danger of imposing your ready-made solution regardless of the problem.

Notes

1 A term used for multiple choice evaluation sheets given out at the end of a course, covering content, accommodations, presenter, etc ranked on a scale from completely unsatisfied to completely satisfied.

2 Deutsche Post DHL is the world's leading mail and logistics services group. The Deutsche Post and DHL corporate brands represent a one-of-a-kind portfolio of logistics (DHL) and communications (Deutsche Post) services. The Group provides its customers with both easy-to-use standardized products as well as innovative and tailored solutions ranging from dialog marketing to industrial supply chains. About 480,000 employees in more than 220 countries and territories form a global network focused on service, quality and sustainability. Where programs in the areas of environmental protection, disaster management and education, the Group is committed to social responsibility. In 2013, Deutsche Post DHL generated revenues of more than 55 billion euros. *The* postal service for Germany. *The* logistics company for the world.

3 A process development invented by Reg Revans in the late 1960s where groups of peers solve their own problems by focusing on asking questions and owning actions that emerge from the discussions.

4 Jivesoftware.com provides social management software for enterprises. It allows companies to build online communities to share knowledge and insights.

5 MOOC stands for 'massive online open courses' and was set up in the United States by universities offering free courses to hundreds of thousands of students using online video and text resources and peer-marked or computer-marked assignments. Courses typically last about 12 weeks and are entirely open: anyone can sign up.

PART TWO
New Ideas for Learning

What 70:20:10 is and why it is important

Introduction

This chapter examines the workplace learning methodology called 70:20:10. Its name represents the rough percentage allocations of different types of learning in any organization at any time. Although we tend to focus on the 10 per cent (formal courses), the other 90 per cent (informal and on-the-job learning) are equally important and often make the formal learning more successful and certainly more impactful. Therefore, the key message is *not* that the three categories of learning described neatly divide into those exact percentage allocations. No one has yet proved this and it is not significant. Rather, the model demonstrates a continuum of learning that stretches from learning integrated into work practice, through related reflection and discussion, to learning that is formal and separate from work. A good learning leader pays attention to and tries to optimize all three.

This chapter explains the model in detail and examines its implications for workplace learning with probably the world's leading 70:20:10 expert, Charles Jennings. There are a number of ways in which corporate learning operations can embrace the model and these are discussed and defined.

What is 70:20:10?

Fundamentally it is a model that challenges assumptions about the role of the learning leader, as much as anything else. By implication it forces any learning team to explore the context in which learning takes place, and encourages them to exploit the extensive opportunities for learning embedded in the day-to-day practice of work so as to maximize the opportunities for skill development and behaviour change. It therefore shifts the emphasis away from the development and deployment of catalogues of courses to the development and deployment of great learning environments that encourage and enable learning to take place anywhere; in other words, developing a culture within the workplace that merges work and learning.

Although much of the model is well known, and there has been a lot of talk about social and informal learning (see, in particular, Cross, 2008) the systematic application of the model is less well discussed, in spite of the fact that many large companies in a range of sectors have embraced its logic. The rigorous implementation of 70:20:10 fundamentally changes the role of the learning team and the role of learning in organizations. It encourages the learning team to deliver everything that they do in the context of work, and the model assumes that the output of learning is measured not by how successful a particular learning event has been but by how far its impact has rippled out into on-the-job behaviours. It connects learning at a fundamental level to business performance. This is an integrated, holistic and dynamic model that holds much promise for the future.

Why we need to think beyond courses

The era of equating corporate learning with the delivery of a portfolio of courses is almost consigned to history. There are four compelling reasons for this:

1 The pace of change in most organizations far outstrips the ability of the learning team to develop and deliver new courses.

2 Neuroscience tells us, in ever more strident terms, that a course, on its own, will not deliver the behaviour changes necessary to embed learning into practice. Without this behavioural change much investment in learning is wasted, and staff are not equipped to keep pace with the changing needs of their customers and the more and more complex demands placed on them by their organizations.

3 Courses, on their own, will not create a learning organization or empower staff to take control of their own learning. The dotting of courses throughout the calendar year tends to isolate learning from work and creates insufficient opportunity to learn or meet the changing needs of the organization. It also creates a perception that learning is someone else's problem. It separates out the need to share

knowledge from the learning process and builds a dependency culture: here I am, train me! We need new ways of thinking about learning and new models to apply learning in organizations: 70:20:10 is a new way of thinking about learning at work.

4   The distribution and deployment of a formal course catalogue absolves virtually everybody, apart from the learning team, from taking any kind of responsibility for the learning process. This includes the executive decision makers, line managers and the individuals who will take the programmes. It is someone else's role to make this work. If you want learning efficiency and effectiveness within a company, all of these people need to take a degree of responsibility and feel ownership of the process.

What is the debate about 70:20:10?

This model for learning and development was, originally, formally outlined by Lombardo and Eichinger (1996). In its simplest form it states that, in any given organization, roughly 70 per cent of learning takes place on-the-job, a further 20 per cent is derived from feedback, experience and learning from example, and the remaining 10 per cent comprises formal courses or reading.

You can trace these ideas further back to the adult learning research conducted by the Canadian Academic Allen Tough in Toronto during the late 1960s. He showed that the vast majority of adult learning is informal and self-directed rather than based on formal learning programmes (Tough, 1971). Only a small percentage of adults' learning stems from formal learning environments or formal courses, although the formal courses can stimulate more informal learning activities. He based this research on extensive interviews that he conducted with adults in the Toronto area.

The proponents of the model have been challenged to explain where the empirical evidence for making such stark percentage claims about different types of learning has come from. Anyone working in corporate learning knows, instinctively, that those three areas embrace work-based learning, and that the proportions indicated are 'reasonable' even if the exact percentages cannot be proved.

When individual companies have attempted to categorize their learning, the results tend to mirror the ratios above and no one disagrees that those three components are the correct ones. So, in many ways, a focus on whether we are talking about 70:20:10 or 65:10:25 completely misses the point.

The issue is, quite simply, that concentrating only on optimizing the smallest element, ie formal courses, crucially leaves out a number of things, such as the opportunity to integrate learning across an organization, and the chance to optimize and improve most of the learning that goes on in an organization beyond the scope and reach of the small percentage that can be linked to formal courses. Clearly, the need to learn, and our capacity to learn, far exceeds what can be provided in the occasional course, whether online or face-to-face.

The advent of Google and YouTube has brought this into stark reality. If anyone wants to learn how to build pivot tables in Excel, for example, the last thing on their mind is a formal face-to-face course which they may have to wait weeks to access. Nick Shackleton-Jones (see Chapter 3) captures this in a tweet sent from the Learning Technologies conference in January 2014: 'I don't know anyone who, if they wanted to put up shelves in autumn, would take a DIY class in spring.' What they would do is make a cursory Google search on the day, and discover a huge number of well-structured short video clips that can be accessed on demand, bookmarked and returned to again and again. And this core learning at the moment of need is delivered at no cost to the user. In this instance, the informal learning approach has totally replaced formal learning.

Charles Jennings

One of the key proponents of 70:20:10 is Charles Jennings. He is a former global learning leader at Reuters, later Thomson Reuters. He espoused the model and developed it in his company and has since worked with many other companies and government organizations, using 70:20:10 as a framework.

Charles uses as evidence to support the model a survey in Edinburgh of 206 leaders and managers carried out by Good Practice's Peter Casebow and Owen Ferguson, that affirmed the learning split that Lombardo and Eichinger found 15 years previously (Casebow and Ferguson, 2010). Jennings quotes from the survey:

> Informal chats with colleagues were the most frequent development activity used by managers (and one of the two activities seen as being most effective – the other one being on-the-job instruction from a manager or colleague).
> 82 per cent of those surveyed said that they would consult a colleague at least once a month, and 83 per cent rated this way as very or fairly effective as

a means of helping them perform in their role when faced with an unfamiliar challenge. The other top most frequently used manager development activities included search, trial and error, and other professional resources.

At a conference that I attended in October 2012 (Masie Learning, Orlando) packed with learning professionals, someone from the stage asked the audience how they go about learning something new. Google and YouTube were the most popular answers. If the problem was work-based, the response was to ask a colleague. Far down the list came 'enrol on a course'. It is highly unlikely that the 1,500 or so learning professionals gathered together that day were very different from the population at large. This does not make courses irrelevant, it simply puts them in their rightful place!

The 70:20:10 model has been quietly gaining traction. Large and small organizations have found it helpful in moving their learning organization forward. Apart from Thomson Reuters, countless other companies such as adidas, Novartis, Diageo, Lego, Boston Scientific and Microsoft have moved in this direction. It is now inconceivable that someone in charge of learning for a large corporation would not have heard of this model or not be actively looking at its implications for his or her company. In spite of the lack of definitive empirical evidence to endorse the model, it now has a traction and a credibility that are indisputable.

The model in detail

In discussing 70:20:10 with Charles Jennings, I drilled down into the model in a little more detail. Charles is now the managing director of Duntroon Associates and runs the global 70:20:10 Forum. His work is more and more concerned with helping organizations think through the implications of 70:20:10 and, indeed, begin the implementation process. As the 70:20:10 Forum grows, it is unlikely that this will change. He tends now to talk not about '70' but *experience,* not about '20' but *exposure,* and not about '10' but *education.* The shift in thinking, however, goes beyond establishing a balance between those three components and dedicating time to optimizing the contribution of each to the overall learning mix.

The essential focus should be one step back from that: trying to understand how high performers working in an organization became and remain high performers. Once this is understood it is possible to encourage more and more staff to raise their performance level as well. The focus is, therefore, not on learning but on building high-performance cultures. In other words learning is, crucially, no longer an end in itself (a social good) but a means to an end (better business performance). We have to think beyond courses and beyond processes, to what impacts performance either positively or negatively. The model's ultimate aim is to build a self-sustaining culture of continuous development. It is a way of thinking about the relationship between performance and learning that is both provocative and challenging. The learning leader's role is much more about facilitating the 70:20:10 model and ensuring that all of its components are closely linked and work together, than it is to deliver courses.

This model, according to Jennings' definition, does not focus on three separate components of learning in organizations. The focus is on making learning work better and increasing its impact: the three components are points along a continuum of related areas of work-based development. The most important role of a learning leader is to ensure that the three components articulate with one another to create maximum impact. This is a fundamental rethink of how you manage learning in organizations. If you like, instead of putting learning *into* work (which is what a course essentially is) you extract learning *from* work and ensure it is accessible and shared.

This model easily embraces a number of other key activities that could have previously been seen as beyond the scope of the learning team, such as informal learning, performance support, and learning through stretch assignments and short-term projects. As these other areas become larger components of growing and developing people at work, this model becomes more resilient and logical.

The model operates best in a dynamic, changing work environment that requires individuals to become increasingly flexible and adaptable. It implies a culture of continuous learning, inseparable from the work process, as well as an almost instinctive sharing of insight and knowledge. It is an output not an input model, which looks at how each component impacts on the performance of the individual and by extension the performance of the organization.

It works with the grain, making what 'naturally' occurs in any organization – on-the-job learning, offering advice and sharing experience – articulate with more formal and structured learning processes. The learning team has to facilitate and organize not only access to courses assembled by a dedicated team, but access to resources, to people and to knowledge as it is churned and created on a day-to-day basis. If you can sustain a continuous process of knowledge and skills acquisition and share that across the workplace, you have the essence of a learning organization and, by extension, the essence of a high-performing culture.

CASE STUDY   Induction in BP

The oil company BP decided to build a series of online resources rather than offer a formal, fixed induction course for its new starters. The resources were intranet-based and allowed new staff to explore many aspects of the company and its work. Depending on need or circumstance, starters could get a quick overview of facets of the company, or dive deeply into business areas. Linked with the information were people who could be contacted as part of the induction process, and a record of the subsequent learning journey could be shared with line managers. The programme met the needs of disparate individuals going into disparate careers, but also met the changing needs of individuals as they began their working life within the company. Induction sat alongside work, not as an adjunct. It went along with individuals on their BP journey and could solve multiple issues at multiple times: just enough at just the right moment.

This highly efficient outcome was substantially cheaper than running a formal induction programme. It met more needs more simply, and integrated longitudinally into the workflow. The early evaluation of the programme indicated large numbers of new staff accessing the resource and satisfaction with the learning outcomes. This high regard came from those individuals on the programme and their line managers as well. It was also a resource for the entire company offering information at the moment of need: more than a third of the company has accessed the site to explore or discover.

Induction therefore changed from being two or three unfocused and general days at the beginning of a work career into a performance support guide that could stay with the employee as his or her career evolved and the job changed. It had the added benefit of being available to anyone in the company should they need new insight or information as their job role evolved or their role changed. Furthermore, it highlighted where expertise was located across the company, or gave contact information for experts in a particular area. For a company like BP it made a lot of sense, delivered better outcomes, and saved money.

The implications for workplace learning

Charles Jennings thinks that the increased focus on social and on-the-job workplace learning is causing 'considerable disruption in the L&D world' (Jennings, 2012). He goes on to claim that it is not just those in:

'traditional roles... who are designers and deliverers of courses and programs, but also to the whole ecosystem of training and learning suppliers that inhabit the L&D world providing programs, courses and content... as well as the supporting infrastructure to deliver... events.

The key message is that practice, reflection and context are vital ingredients for effective learning and the need to rehearse and explore the learning is the only way to ensure that what is developed in the 'lab' or the classroom translates effectively back into the workplace. This is not a new idea: Kidd (1971, 1973) pointed out that learning by adults was not usually an isolated phenomenon but happened in a specific cultural or social context. This helps explain why much investment in development can fail. If you remove the context, what sounds compelling in the lecture theatre (ie away from the working environment in which it will be applied), could be difficult to translate satisfactorily into the workplace. The minute the participant tries to implement what has been learnt he or she is confronted by the culture of the organization, or 'the way we do things around here'. Any learning programme that puts an emphasis on behaviour change or culture change and offers support that takes account of the organization's resistance to change in the context of the real work environment, is going to be more effective than one that ignores these things.

It is also true that we learn through experience. The organization that offers carefully structured experiences to stretch and test employees will increase their competence and performance. The filmmaker David Puttnam, now Lord Puttnam, once told me that he would deliberately give his best staff assignments that would keep them awake at night worrying about how they would deliver. He claimed that these will always be the most rewarding and most developmental of assignments. They took the individuals concerned to a higher level of performance from which they never looked back. To work effectively, and to benefit the entire organization, stretch assignments need careful consideration and measured support and should be widely offered, not delivered by the occasional gifted leader.

The chief executive of the US conglomerate General Electric, Jeffrey Immelt, as an up-and-coming executive in its chemicals division, was given the task of sorting out a major manufacturing crisis in the company by the CEO at the time, Jack Welch. Immelt had no direct experience of its consumer white goods manufacturing sector, yet he was put in charge of solving a major problem concerning the failure of compressors in a large number of domestic refrigerators. Having to work on that problem and resolve it to the satisfaction of both the company and its customers was a defining moment in Immelt's career development. This was a task deliberately given to him by Jack Welch as a massive stretch assignment.

Learning projects are not just directed by managers in the workplace. As the former academic Allen Tough demonstrated, through research conducted over 40 years ago, adults undertake at least one or two, and often 15 or 20 self-directed learning projects every year. This is part of being human and a normal reaction to complex challenges in complex environments. Some of these are, or could obviously be, work based (Tough, 1971). Part of any programme of staff development ought, therefore, to encourage a number of work-based projects initiated by the company or the individual.

In many ways we are playing a game of perpetual catch-up as we try to make learning at work more effective and more resonant. It is useful to bring adult learning research and discoveries in neuroscience to bear on this. These are small indicators of a significant sea-change in what we consider to be the appropriate role and direction for L&D.

What you can do

Charles Jennings has written a number of papers and publications on the 70:20:10 model. In terms of the '70' element of the model (on-the-job or experiential learning) he suggests:

- Providing the chance to work as a member of a small team.
- Identifying opportunities to reflect and learn from projects.
- Directly intervening after a formal learning programme to create opportunities to immediately apply new learning and new skills in real situations.
- Specifically building a new role or adding to an existing one in a systematic way.
- Building assignments that provide broad, holistic experience.

I would add to this list:

- Develop a job role in stages so that the individual can build on each developmental stage to create a more complex and holistic role.
- In the early stages of undertaking a new job, expect and even demand that learning is built into the process.
- Expect less performance in the early stages of undertaking a new job and encourage more conscious reflection on how the job works.
- Create opportunities for access to performance support resources.

- Gradually extend the range of autonomy given to an individual as he or she takes on more responsibility and gains competence.
- Offer plenty of feedback so that the learning on-the-job has clear outcomes and the performance levels expected are clearly identified.
- Build in time for discussion on a regular basis so that the individual can work out what has been achieved and what still needs to be undertaken.

Much of this is in common practice, but it often occurs through happenstance rather than being systematically planned for or seen as an integral part of the culture. It is often applied randomly in an organization, so that one team with, say, a sympathetic manager, is allowed to progress further down this route than a team with a less sympathetic manager. Often the good practice exists somewhere; it simply needs to be captured and systematized and built into 'the way we do things around here'.

For the '20' element of the model (informal learning/experience), Jennings suggests:

- Establish a culture of coaching from managers/colleagues/others.
- Encourage advice seeking, or general sounding out for ideas and support.
- Engage in formal and informal mentoring.
- Support professionalism in industry association membership and external networking.
- Create a culture of action learning.

I would add:

- Guarantee employees at least one stretch project per year, perhaps more.
- Always gather feedback on those projects so that the learning is embedded.
- Set up Communities of Practice so that staff with common areas of expertise can pool their knowledge.
- Make it an expectation of senior or experienced staff that they share their knowledge when asked, and build that into the framework of their working week or month.
- Make team debriefs good learning experiences rather than reward and punishment sessions.
- Offer the staff, as far as possible, opportunities to see how their career could develop.

- Make part of the managers' role the need to spend time on regular feedback and regular coaching of the team.

- Encourage sharing and teamwork. This should be the norm rather than the exception.

- Support proactive conversations between managers and team members so that somebody in the early stages of a career or early into a new role is asked regularly how they are doing, rather than the manager waiting for the individual to ask for help.

- Accept that small failures are a part of that learning process and treat them as such.

The 70:20:10 model takes us on a trajectory away from self-directed, disconnected learning teams who manage catalogues of courses and see the development or delivery of those courses to be the entirety of their role. Instead, learning becomes organization-wide and the learning team's role is much more focused on building and managing successful learning environments that put the learner at the centre of the process. Charles Jennings calls them 'workscapes' or work/learning environments. The aim is to focus on impact and performance rather than numbers of courses or customer satisfaction.

How that learning emerges is less important than its effectiveness. It is hard to imagine any company that is moving in this direction remaining satisfied with 'happy sheets' and course directories. It is also hard to imagine that the learning team would not be out there in the workplace speaking the language of the business and engaging with it directly.

Charles Jennings sums up this process in three key tasks. The first is to support the workplace learning process. The second is to help the workforce improve their learning skills and provide them with tools that enable learning. The third is to create a supportive organizational culture that encourages learning, debate, discussion and constant mentoring and coaching. The learning leader has to embrace all three areas, not one or two.

One of the most innovative companies of our age is Google. At the end of 2005, its former chief executive and now chairman, Eric Schmidt, articulated a 70:20:10 model for managing innovation in the company. This enshrined the much debated '10 per cent time' offered to Google engineers to work on their own projects. Schmidt defined this model as an allocation of 70 per cent of work time to core business task and 20 per cent on projects related to the core business, allowing the remaining 10 per cent of time for projects unrelated to the core business. He assumed that most innovation would come from that 10 per cent free time (Battelle, 2005). The proof of that pudding is in the number of substantive Google projects that have emerged from that 10 per cent time: Google Earth, Googlemail and even the advertising keywords idea that is the core element of the company's revenue.

Schmidt's innovation model is not the same as the 70:20:10 learning model but there are many overlapping elements. Both believe that great ideas emerge from the workflow when given space. And both believe that an injection of new ideas (or new skills) comes from the systematic application of a universal model that is built into the culture of the organization rather than relying on the discretion of individual managers or occasional formal events.

Next steps

To support the workplace learning process you first have to understand what it is. You do this not by auditing the number of courses or the number of learners who take those courses, but by auditing learning within your workplace. This involves gathering attitudes about learning from across the organization: how easy access is, what barriers exist that prevent uptake, and what is the general cultural attitude towards a focus on developing new skills and competences.

There are many ways to undertake this kind of audit but they mostly involve interviewing or surveying staff. If the first means of data collection is a survey, small numbers of staff drawn from across the organization need to be interviewed in more depth, to validate or challenge that survey data. Areas to explore include:

- how critical learning has been in doing your job well;
- the attitude of the organization when you attempt to learn;
- the barriers put in place to prevent learning;
- the amount of support given;
- the amount of follow-through;
- the ease with which mentoring opportunities can be accessed for both mentor and mentee;
- the encouragement given to implementing new learning within the workflow;
- the perception within the organization about the opportunities for career development and the broadening of job roles.

In any survey, the more questions you ask the fewer responses you will receive, so strike a balance between gathering useful data and creating too great a time burden that acts as a disincentive to respond. Six or seven questions are usually adequate for achieving productive results.

From the survey you will get a much clearer idea of how learning works inside other organizational processes and the workflow, not in theory but in practice. On the basis of that there will be a number of fundamental tasks that have to be addressed and you will need a strategy for each of them. Although these are often cultural issues, with the right strategy you can make good progress in a matter of months. To thoroughly embed these changes will take much longer.

The second task is to help the workforce improve their learning skills and provide them with tools that enable learning. This sounds more straightforward than it actually is. Work is all about performance, so it is often hard to create the space for learning about learning. If enabling more direct work-based programmes is difficult to justify, then what some may consider abstract concepts are almost impossible to build upon and develop. So, you do not help the workforce improve learning skills by running learning skill courses. This is best achieved through sharing stories from the best learners in the organization, and attempting to establish them as role models. It also requires the development or delivery of good resources that are easily accessible. This can be job-based material or more generic, but it has to be freely accessible. If you make resources available, you quietly encourage a shift towards independent learning. It helps too, to offer personal online space for each staff member to store relevant articles, book summaries, insights and other material. This kind of storage is cheap and companies could realistically offer gigabytes of storage to every employee; unfortunately many do not. There are many ways of extending access to resources. Ask yourself what improvements offer the greatest potential for cultural change at the lowest possible cost. Thomson Reuters brought in Books 24-7 (online business book summaries) in an attempt to stimulate curiosity and informal learning, as well as offering useful work-related resources. The massive uptake indicated that the workforce had a great thirst for learning and a desire to do things better that had, up until that point, been largely unmet.

The third task is to help capture personal development and ensure that discussions about personal development are part of a performance review and actively encouraged and logged.

The fourth is to create a supportive organizational culture that encourages learning, debate, discussion and constant mentoring and coaching. Building a supportive culture is a slow process and involves support from the highest levels within an organization. Without the endorsement and encouragement of senior executives, it is highly unlikely that the cultural change you wish to encourage will ever occur. It is therefore critical that you gain endorsement and sponsorship from the senior management team before attempting to move forward. Even at an early stage in this process, a statement alone is not as impressive as a statement backed by decisive action.

Sometimes role models can help show what can be achieved or what is required. It is all part of modelling the change you wish to see, and showing rather than telling individual staff members what this is about. If you can model what the future may look like, what will be achieved and when, you can build up expectations. If this is coupled with clear indications of what direct support or resources individuals can expect, this dramatically helps move things forward.

In addition to senior managers, line managers and supervisors must be deeply involved. Their direct contact with staff can reinforce or undermine any number of statements or gestures. If they are not on board, it can appear as if the organization is offering something with one hand and taking it back with the other. In this case, a high level of cynicism develops which can often set the whole process back beyond the point where you started.

To develop any kind of trajectory, it is important that you make an accurate analysis of what is really going on in the organization. This will help you to begin to map out the critical and realistic steps to move from where you are to where it is desirable (or even essential) to be. Each workplace is different and each group of staff has different aspirations, but the simple mantra of 'backed by action, based on evidence' is the essential ingredient.

Conclusions

Embracing the 70:20:10 model is not an audit process where you count the learning and hope that you are within its parameters. It is a process of steadily extending the scope of learning and building a climate where what is delivered formally is more than matched by a range of informal learning opportunities that are not managed but allowed to develop everywhere. It is this climate of maximizing and embedding what formal learning can offer, together with allowing and encouraging learning and development issues to be picked up and resolved by staff, which generates a climate of ideas and knowledge sharing.

The model could be the key to unlocking the fundamental building blocks of a learning organization where most learning operates independently of the learning team and where the distinction between conversation, support, coaching, mentoring and learning has long faded. It is a challenge worth taking seriously. Many companies, such as Shell, Philips, Maersk, GAP, Nike and American Express are moving in this direction. So could you.

Measuring impact

Introduction

One of the strongest indicators of how things have changed in learning is the fact that impact measurement warrants a chapter of its own. Not very many years ago it was possible to spend a long and successful career in L&D without ever really considering the impact your operation was making on the organization that employed you, apart from the obvious fact that you ran courses and people seemed, for the most part, to enjoy them. That is not to say that evaluation was ignored: data was assiduously collected on every single thing that was delivered. This data explored in great detail the immediate level of satisfaction perceived by the learners for each programme, the minute it finished. There was also a subjective rating given on how useful the programme had been. Beyond that, only the brave few ever ventured, and managers rarely demanded any more.

Traditionally, this form of data collection is known as 'happy sheets'. Students were invited to rate their instructor, the teaching room, even the food they were served on a five-point scale. This capture of participants' immediate reaction to the learning experience is owed largely to the work of Professor Donald L Kirkpatrick from the University of Wisconsin, who first published his Four-level Training Evaluation Method in 1959, based on his PhD thesis that was submitted to the university in 1954.

Kirkpatrick never intended all the focus to be on his first level: 'reaction'; he wanted evaluation to encompass all the levels from 'reaction' through 'learning' to 'behaviour' then 'impact'. As each stage got more difficult to measure accurately, it was 'reaction' that stuck. All of the reaction data is normally collected immediately after the programme ends, and at the point where participants are rushing to get home – not the ideal circumstances for thoughtful or reflective comments. It is used to compile a list of courses ranked by their popularity, enjoyment and usefulness to their cohort, and is an insurance policy against learning disasters. The problem was, it told us nothing about the impact of learning beyond the immediate and the superficial.

At no point did anyone collect data on what happened to that learning once it transitioned back into the workplace and into the day-to-day working environment. Whether anything changed, whether processes became more efficient or whether anyone else in that environment noticed a difference in the behaviour or activity of the participant was completely ignored. Even this limited data rarely got distributed beyond the learning team and even then only as high-level summaries. Phrases such as 'Learner numbers increased by 4.5 per cent and learner satisfaction remained very high' were commonplace. The limited nature of these data sets did not mean that everything that was delivered was a waste of time or that no impact was achieved. The simple fact was that no one was able to judge apart from by anecdote or hearsay. They had no information apart from rumour and, it has to be said, no one asked for more.

In many ways, L&D flourished (and suffered) from indifference. It was always 'nice to have' and that gave the delivery team a lot of flexibility and leeway. If it was nice to have, it didn't much matter what it was that you had. If learning was generally 'good' in the organization, the fact that it existed was more important than whether it did anything in particular. This allowed a certain kind of culture to flourish and, in many places, it allowed a lot of innovation to quietly emerge. However, it also encouraged what Charles Jennings called 'the conspiracy of convenience' (in a presentation at Learning Technologies 2012), by which he meant a complacent and sticking-plaster approach to L&D. When performance was poor in a part of the organization, the manager in charge of that area could avoid any deep analysis by asking for 'training'. The training manager, seeing an opportunity to engage with the business, delivered a programme that appeared to address that deficit or problem. No one measured what took place, apart from gathering Kirkpatrick's 'reaction' sheets. Evidence of business impact was ignored, and yet the operational manager felt that he or she had done something and the training manager felt that he or she had responded to a business need. Everyone was happy and nothing much changed. The training manager had played a decisive role in the business; the operational manager had addressed a problem. It was in no one's interests to probe much further.

The lack of deep commitment to L&D also meant that whenever times were tough, it was a safe and easy budget to cut. The number of staff employed in

L&D, as well as the number of learning programmes, went up and down as it tracked the business cycle. As nothing much appeared to suffer when cuts were made it was an easy decision; and as learning was generally popular it was an easy decision to restore a budget when it was safe and affordable to do so. This feast and famine cycle continued for decades.

What changed it was, in part, the global financial crisis in 2008. At this point, savage cuts were made to many L&D operations around the world. Indeed, many departments were entirely disbanded or reduced to a skeleton staff with minimal budgets. In some ways this was the consequence of a disconnected L&D that Kirkpatrick had predicted in the 1950s[1] when he warned of 'the philanthropic attitude' to training being taken for granted. When things improved, however, it was a different approach and model that came back into the workplace. At this point, 'What do I get for my money?' became the key question in many instances, and the simple message attached to it was: 'Please provide an answer or leave!' Those who rose to that challenge were able to create more embedded and accountable L&D operations, and once they focused on that question it changed how they managed them.

Today, there is a crescendo of voices demanding to know 'What do I get for my money?' This may be a simple question but it reflects a fundamental change of philosophy and accountability. This chapter has been written to help you answer that question. Increasingly, unless you can answer with some degree of certainty, nothing much else that you do will really matter.

Robert Brinkerhoff, the evaluation guru, argues that if failed execution is behind most businesses' lack of success, it should follow that the role of L&D is to accelerate the implementation of strategy by delivering the 'skills, knowledge and actions that accelerate execution of necessary strategic change' (Brinkerhoff, 2013). Consequently the role of evaluation should be to measure the effectiveness of that process and of the execution itself. Learning, if it is correctly aligned and focused, is a critical part of business rather than a staff benefit that is 'nice to have' that makes no fundamental difference in the day-to-day process of work.

The Business Success Case Method

This chapter looks at one particular model of impact measurement, the Business Success Case Method, which is gaining traction. It is not the only answer, but it does outline the main components of how you build a framework that genuinely responds to the need to quantify the impact your programme has made in the achievement of your organization's targets. It helps in acquiring the right mindset and approach and it can be easily adapted.

The method is not an exact science and workplaces are messy, but it does take us a long way down the path of establishing frameworks that will generate sufficient data for unambiguous statements about the problem that the learning was intended to solve and the overall impact of the L&D strategy that has been brought to bear. It can also match that impact with the investment that was made in the programme, and offer tangible data on the effectiveness, efficiency and the contribution to profitability of a specific learning programme, the learning in a department or even the learning impact for the company as a whole. This is a prize worth striving for.

CASE STUDY   Kenneth Fee, Airthrey Ltd

Kenneth Fee is co-author of a recent e-book on evaluating learning (Fee and Rutherford, 2012) and the owner of an evaluation consultancy called Airthrey Ltd. He has established an online subscriber evaluation community to support evaluation initiatives worldwide, the Learning Evaluation Network (**www.learningevaluationnetwork.ning.com**). What I wanted to know was why he thought evaluation was an increasingly big issue. Fee's view is strongly aligned with the views expressed in this book: if you cannot prove the value of what you do to the business you are in, there is no real justification for doing anything in the first place. Happy sheets have their place: they do track learner engagement, but learner reaction is only one indicator, and an insufficient one to demonstrate impact and value.

Fee believes that even the humble reaction questionnaire could be much more effective if it were prepared with more care, with better questions, and delivered at a more appropriate time. And it could be used to analyse progress and learner impact over successive iterations of a programme, rather than be scanned quickly for any adverse comments and then filed away in a cupboard.

The key issue for Fee is impact, and how you can gather convincing and accurate data on impact that can be shared widely. He has worked with hundreds of L&D professionals to help them build the right model to deliver this in their context, so he does not believe that there is one ultimate model that can be applied in every circumstance and used equally in every organization. What is required, and what he tries to develop, is an evaluation mindset. With that, it is possible to pick the appropriate tools that work in the specific context in which you find yourself. The starting point has to be one very simple question: what value has this intervention delivered to the business? I would add a second: what problem was it trying to solve and did it succeed? You can then work backwards from that. A series of simple but very powerful questions emerge:

1 What were you expecting to happen?

2 What evidence can you gather (qualitative or quantitative) to prove or disprove the outcomes that you expected?

3 Which of your questions or evidence will reward deeper analysis and drilling down?

4 Can you show that any change is a permanent modification of behaviour, not an immediate reaction to the intervention?

5 Can you produce enough evidence to be reasonably sure of your conclusions?

6 Can you frame that evidence in a way that the rest of the organization will understand?

Clearly, it would be inappropriate to address these questions with the same intensity for each programme you run. The key is to select and focus on those with the maximum visibility, or those you or others have some anxieties about in terms of their effectiveness, or you feel have been undervalued in what they have achieved. L&D should own this and be prepared to argue hard for an appropriate intervention. Each programme needs a separate, carefully thought through strategy. Factors that determine what is appropriate include cost of investment, criticality of impact, numbers involved and complexity of programme.

Fee believes that it is actually counterproductive to measure everything. You should focus on what matters and use statistically significant sampling. Deep analysis of a sample population will always yield more than a comprehensive analysis at a superficial level. A small number of good, well-framed questions asked at the right moment can yield useful data. Swamping participants or their managers with a huge number of questions at varying levels of trivia rarely delivers the same result as a few well-chosen questions. The overwhelming key question is: what changes did we expect to see, and did we see them?

(The annex to Fee and Rutherford's (2012) book contains a comprehensive literature review of learning evaluation that shares with the reader the wide range of models and approaches to learning evaluation, and clarifies the jargon.)

Key points

This process is really a significant change in approach and attitude and I would sum it up in 10 key points:

1 Take the advice of Jack Phillips[2] and be liberal with your allocation of costs and conservative in embracing benefits. Claiming full credit for a performance upturn is rarely realistic or sensible; an agreed percentage of the credit is usually much more acceptable. When you look at costs, it is often helpful to add in the full costs, including time involved, set against those benefits. Remember that benefits accrue over time: you do not have to prove the value of an intervention within weeks of it having taken place. Do not do all the estimating yourself: colleagues outside L&D are often best placed to allocate the degree of the contribution towards a successful strategy.

2 Never define the impact of a programme the day after the last person has completed it. It can take several months to establish whether there has been a change in behaviour that leads to lasting improved performance. Agree with senior executives what a realistic timescale might be.

3 Do not take credit for building 'enjoyable' programmes. Sometimes it is necessary to create a level of discomfort for relearning to take place. A baseline of competent delivery should be taken for granted and not seen as a source of praise and achievement.

4 You need a clear picture of where you are now and where you want to be, to have any hope of building an effective evaluation strategy. Evaluation must start *before* delivery, not after.

5 Baselines can be generic. A staff survey can yield vital information, and marketing data from customers can create significant opportunities to define skills and performance deficits. For example, PWC, the consultancy, uses some of the data from its global people survey for L&D impact measurement. Do not reinvent: reuse and repurpose.

6 Do not try too hard to ring-fence the impact of L&D. This can isolate the function from complex business processes; some acknowledgement of other factors is sensible and accurate.

7 Always check that the evidence you are going to use is acceptable as a measure before you use it. This means sharing your strategy with people outside L&D before you implement it. For example, if you are using marketing data, discuss and gain approval from those who own it before using it to draw conclusions.

8 Recognize that what matters most to the organization is not what matters most to you and your team. Your function is to do what is necessary to come up with verifiable conclusions rather than what is easy to gather or that paints a convenient picture.

9 Always think in terms of business issues. Speak the language of business. Frame your analysis in business terms. Have conversations with those at the sharp end. Check that what you are saying makes sense to them.

10 Pilot your evaluation strategies and your reporting model. Work out what is necessary to achieve 'roughly reasonable data'[3] that gives you an arguable confidence about claiming specific impact.

A final cautionary tale to add here: do not attempt to measure everything and every programme at the same level of intensity. Focus on what is biggest or most important. You cannot do everything, so it is important that you pick your subjects and your areas for debate and discussion. Get those decisions ratified so you know that these are the right areas. You are quantifying what value you are adding to the business; you are not attempting to justify the existence of an L&D department!

Thinking about evaluation in a different way

Learning and development interventions only make an impact when the necessary knowledge and skills acquired by individuals to move an organization in a particular direction end with appropriate changed behaviour and action that is tangible and measurable. That said, the record of L&D in changing behaviour is not stellar. Ron Brinkerhoff's research (Brinkerhoff and Mooney, 2008) indicates that in many instances, in numerous different sectors, out of 100 learners 20 do not even attempt to apply the learning; 65 try to some extent but give up; leaving only 15 on whom learning has a significant and lasting impact. The unrealized value of that development investment is therefore massive. If, for example, you could get a 90 per cent transfer rate rather than a 15 to 20 per cent, your return on investment would be massively more than the generic return indicated by Brinkerhoff's research, and that would give you a distinct competitive advantage.

Brinkerhoff argues that by starting out with impact in mind, you can achieve transfer rates of up to 90 per cent. The implication of this is that evaluating the training at Kirkpatrick level 1 (reaction) is virtually pointless, as any indication of learner satisfaction has little to do with implementing changed behaviour over time. The key is to look at a complex process that begins before any learning event and continues beyond it. Responsibility for impact cannot simply be delegated to the L&D department or blamed on the quality of a learning event. Impact measurement requires the intentional involvement of senior managers and line managers and demands their full engagement and commitment throughout the process. In fact, the whole organization is ultimately accountable. Managers have to engage continuously with the L&D operation and see it as a critical part of their own oversight and an operational tool to help deliver their own targets.

A good L&D operation spends time working with those key managers so that they will, in turn, focus on ensuring that their staff achieve the maximum impact from any learning intervention. The learner is clearly a critical player in this equation! But he or she is not expected to carry the burden of execution on his or her own. Managers and learners need to discuss an action plan, and the manager should provide coaching and support to ensure its successful implementation. The critical focus is, therefore, on what actually happens after the learning event and back in the workplace. There will be clear expectations defined and careful support and monitoring to ensure that behaviours change and the new skills and attitudes reinvigorate work practice and continue to do so over time.

Key L&D staff are on hand as councillors, facilitators and consultants. They watch what is going on, support the manager and measure impact going forward. Their role does not end when the training event finishes. They have to be as committed to delivering the maximum impact on the business as the manager is. L&D success depends on that transfer ratio of learnt skills and behaviours back into the workplace, and the critical point they need to focus on is how to sustain the use of these skills and changed behaviours over time or until they become automatic.

This is a very different model from one that only measures the success of a learning event by the enjoyment of the participants in a one-off exercise. This model puts L&D at the heart of execution and delivery, and aligns its performance closely with the performance of the business. There is no better place to be or better indicator of success! The mission of the L&D function is not to do great L&D but rather to help the company get great results from its investment in L&D.

The Brinkerhoff approach explained

Robert Brinkerhoff has been talking about impact measurement of training for a long time. In his last book, *Courageous Training* (Brinkerhoff and Mooney, 2008) he focuses on delivering learning that is designed to deliver high impact. It is more about the bigger context in which learning is implemented.

Brinkerhoff (2006) takes us on the three-stage journey from learner reactions, through a change in on-the-job behaviours by individuals, to the overall impact of development on business performance. To do this, he elaborates a six-stage decision cycle, which begins before any intervention is delivered and continues long after the specific training programme has ceased:

1 Goals for the development programme that are worthwhile to the organization are established.

2 A workable programme design is created.

3 The programme design is implemented and made to work.

4 Recipients emerge with new skills, knowledge and attitudes. Establish that enough development has taken place.

5 The recipients use their new skills, knowledge and attitude in their job and in their personal life. These positive reactions are sustained.

6 The use of the new skills, knowledge and attitude benefits the organization as a whole, and further needs are noticeably diminished.

The first stage is, therefore, about goal setting and establishing what the need is. The second stage is to evaluate the programme design: what will work? The third stage is implementation and answering the question: is it working? The fourth stage is evaluating the immediate outcomes: did they learn it? The fifth stage looks at the endurance of the learning: are they continuing to use it? The final stage examines the payoff: did it make a worthwhile difference to the organization? The core components listed here still inform Brinkerhoff's practice. His mantra is that it is pointless evaluating a learning programme in isolation: the focus of any evaluation should be on how well learning is able to improve business performance over time. And L&D cannot alone be responsible for this. All learning has a context.

At each stage different procedures are relevant. In stage 1, attitude surveys, expert reviews and action research studies can clarify what the need is and double-check the initial analysis. What Brinkerhoff wants is for you to confirm what the issue is, as far as possible, before rushing into developing a learning programme. Often learning is not the solution, just a panacea or a smoke screen to avoid the real problem. Failure of a sales team to sell a product or service does not always indicate the need for more development for the team: it might be a lousy or inappropriate product or service!

To establish stage 4 learning outcomes he suggests self-assessment reports, role-plays, knowledge tests and interviews. There are many ways to establish whether learning has taken place beyond a multiple-choice test that simply reinforces rote learning. How many people take compliance programmes and pass the multiple-choice test and promptly forget everything they learnt as the learning is short term and superficial?

At stage 5, he urges that a broad range of learning impacts are considered. Some are qualitative and some quantitative but each benefit that has accrued should be assessed, in cash terms if possible. The total impact of the benefits should be measured against the costs of delivering the programme and there should be a deliberate attempt to review to what extent the initial need has been met.

Brinkerhoff believes that his six-stage model should be used 'no matter how partially or briefly' (Brinkerhoff and Mooney, 2008: 234) as that begins to yield data across the whole span and this will maximize the intended outcomes. He sums up by claiming that: 'The tragedy will come if HRD truly deserves to thrive but is unable to convincingly justify its existence in a competitive corporate environment' (Brinkerhoff and Mooney, 2008: 6). To some extent it has taken over 25 years for the need to prove value in that competitive corporate environment to emerge.

Brinkerhoff's Success Case Method

Brinkerhoff's thinking about evaluation continued to evolve. In early 2000 he coined the phrase 'Success Case Method' (SCM). Brinkerhoff's key insight is that there are many factors that lead to the success or otherwise of a learning intervention. It is therefore important that you take a holistic approach and try to pinpoint all the factors that lead to success (or failure).

Brinkerhoff's SCM is now widely respected and popular around the world and it is worth spending some time discussing it here. This is not to say that other models, notably Jack Phillips ROI model, have no value, but the Brinkerhoff methodology aligns clearly with the broader more holistic approach taken in this book, and it is the one that I would most like to draw to your attention. The philosophy of this book is to situate L&D within the wider context of business; Brinkerhoff does precisely this in his SCM and later work on training for impact.

In *Telling Training's Story: Evaluation made simple, credible and effective*, Brinkerhoff (2006) makes an explicit argument for his SCM. He defines the theory then offers four in-depth case studies that cover a range of development scenarios, from technician and sales training to executive development, that demonstrate his method in action. He reiterates the dominant philosophy that runs all through his work in the preface to the book. It is the theme of this chapter: 'it is clear that we need to provide credible and valid evidence of training impact and show the difference training makes to the bottom line'. He is interested in making clear and unarguable cases that prove investment in people development pays off and contributes to the creation of more successful and more competitive organizations.

Brinkerhoff's philosophy is straightforward. He wants to reduce the complexity of evaluation to simple questions. What did somebody learn? How did they use that learning in their job? And did that use produce a worthwhile outcome? Positive answers to all three questions will help build a convincing case that the investment in development is worthwhile, while negative answers help shape better interventions.

Clearly, to get the answers to these questions you have to ask the people who went through the programme. But it is imperative that you corroborate those answers by collecting evidence from peers and from managers. Any alternative explanations for the change in performance should also be examined so as to isolate, as far as it is possible, the contribution of the development programme, while at the same time acknowledging the complexity of organizational performance issues. Brinkerhoff urges us to understand that: 'training alone is never the sole factor in bringing about improved performance, and is often not even the major contributor. Given this, we never try to make an impact claim for the training alone' (Brinkerhoff, 2006: 7).

The key thing to establish is that the intervention made a difference, while acknowledging other core factors. Sometimes the other factors, such as line manager support, are critical and can be proved to be so. You should start with the idea of delivering maximum impact, and then test your success. That involves building an alliance in the business, negotiating what you want to happen and gaining your allies' support. This all happens before any learning intervention. The critical third stage is supporting the change in behaviour and reinforcing and encouraging that change. So, the most important areas to focus on are the alliance and the impact sought. Those agreements should play a major role in the programme's shape and substance.

Brinkerhoff's method has an explicit goal of indicating what additional factors helped build and deliver the success of the intervention. He does not 'just measure and document the impact of training, but uncovers and pinpoints the factors that make or break training success' (Brinkerhoff, 2006: 6). This information is critical when attempting to build an environment where learning can be successful. It also means that blaming or praising development alone is foolhardy and naive, and also allows others, for example managers, to get off the hook!

Brinkerhoff extrapolates from individual performance to numbers of individuals using the 'roughly reasonable' formula; in other words, how many individuals use their learning and achieve worthwhile outcomes, and what is the value of these outcomes, when added together, to the organization? The essence of the SCM is building a case for learning impact, or lack of impact, one individual at a time. Brinkerhoff does this by interviewing the most and the least successful participants in a given programme. He uses surveys to identify who has been most successful and who has been least successful and the proportions in each category. There is much to learn, Brinkerhoff would argue, from both groups. For example, non-success can be explained by lack of manager support, or success by manager coaching and endorsement. This is nothing to do, necessarily, with the learning programme directly but the context in which the learning takes place.

His method always pinpoints the additional factors that make a contribution to the success of the learning intervention: 'Training is always dependent upon the interaction of these other performance system factors in the improvement of performance' (Brinkerhoff, 2006: 22). He argues that most training programmes have a predictable distribution of impact, ranging from achieving concrete and valuable results to not using the learning at all. To simply average out the performance across the cohort does not identify the real impact of the intervention. Brinkerhoff prefers to look deeply at the highest and lowest performers because they yield the greatest number of lessons about impact.

Brinkerhoff's holistic approach can give managers very good data-based reasons for endorsing learning:

> We can show them specific actions they can take to reinforce learning and performance, and tie these directly to bottom-line results and economic payoff to them and to their organizations. Then, rather than trying to make all sorts of mandatory prescriptions for support actions, we can simply show managers the data and let them do what they are paid to do: look at the facts and make a business decision. (Brinkerhoff, 2006: 7)

Brinkerhoff's research points to the fact that these extrinsic factors often account for more of the success of learning than the elements of the intervention itself. This fact and the body of proof that is marshalled by Brinkerhoff should encourage engaged conversations between L&D staff and executives and managers from outside the development function.

If his logic is understood and accepted, the context in which L&D occurs changes. In reality we are looking at L&D performance that is conditioned by the culture, values and performance management system of the entire organization. Development does not happen in isolation, but in context. That is one of the reasons why Brinkerhoff's work on evaluation has been so important and enduring. The value that an organization receives from a given development intervention is determined by a whole range of factors, many of which are in the organization's control but not directly in the control of the L&D operation.

The SCM process involves a survey; this yields data on the overall distributional of success and non-success. This is followed by an in-depth interview stage. These two parts can be broken down into five steps. The first is to plan the evaluation. The second is to create an impact model that defines potential results and benefits. The third is to design and conduct a survey. The fourth is to conduct in-depth interviews of selected participants from the successful and non-successful ends of the spectrum. Finally, conclusions and recommendations are formulated (Brinkerhoff, 2006: 38).

Brinkerhoff demonstrates that learning alone is insufficient, and learning in isolation cannot be evaluated effectively. It is important to emphasize that learning is not the subject of the evaluation – business impact and leveraging learning are. He explains why the same programmes delivered by the same facilitators in different parts of an organization or in different organizations can have dramatically different impacts. What is highly successful in one place can be a dismal failure in another because: 'Impact from training is a function of a high-quality training intervention that operates in conjunction with a healthy, aligned, and integrated set of performance system factors' (Brinkerhoff, 2006: 44). In other words, the way an organization uses and extends the opportunities delivered by learning to leverage performance is critical to the outcome of a given intervention. In the worst cases the organization is actively impeding the impact of new learning. If you simply focus on the quality of the learning intervention in that instance, you will never get to the bottom of why learning is not working. The SCM can answer a number of broad questions about impact; the key is to understand what questions the organization requires to be answered and use the framework to supply evidence-based answers.

At its core, SCM is a simple impact model that covers the knowledge and skills outcomes; the way in which the new learning is applied in the job; the results that were produced as a consequence; and the broader business goals to which this learning contributed. The structure described here means that, from the very beginning, L&D staff work backwards from the larger business goals, and determine an alignment of new skills and knowledge acquired by an individual to the wider core objectives of the organization as a whole.

The SCM allows the user to answer a number of core questions. Not all of them may be equally relevant in a given evaluation study, but the point is that the whole scope is included in this method. The conclusions range from a specific focus on what the programme delivered through to its contribution to wider business success. Brinkerhoff (2006: 130–31) lists a total of six key evaluation questions:

1 Who used the learning and who did not?

2 When it was used what good did it do?

3 What was the value achieved by those who used it?

4 When it was used, why? Who did what to help make it work?

5 When it was not used, why? Who did (or did not do) what that created obstacles?

6 Who needs to do what to get more people to use their learning successfully?

I added a seventh, which is unavoidable: How do the benefits achieved compare with the costs?

This model, clearly, goes beyond evaluation and begins to suggest an approach and alignment for the entire L&D operation, and helps define the criteria for its success in the context of the organization in which it operates. While Brinkerhoff's model has been 25 years in development, it has really come of age in the last five years. It helps define what the emerging role and status of L&D should and could be. If there is one overall message that Brinkerhoff's work declares loudly and that this chapter reinforces, it is that L&D is far too important to be left exclusively to the L&D team. L&D works most effectively as part of the business with common goals for the business. So, if you really want to maximize the impact of your investment in L&D, the whole business has to be aligned behind any intervention. This is an exciting message for the learning team.

If you want learning to be impactful you need to start with the explicit aim of delivering high-impact programmes and gaining the alliance that will ensure this before you start. Furthermore, the success or failure of the intervention will be determined by the broad engagement of the organization as a whole rather than simply the quality or lack of quality of what is delivered. This is an incredibly important insight and one that is echoed throughout this book.

Ten tips to take this forward

1 You gather alignment around an initiative by talking about the change everyone wants to see in the organization. Iterate this until you are sure you are clear what is required.

2 Start with high impact in mind, and clearly define who is responsible and what it will take. Do not back off this stage: it is worth persevering.

3 Make the learning intervention coherent and exciting and build it beyond just an event. Share success early. Champion those people who make a difference as a result of this intervention.

4 What questions will you ask to determine if you have achieved success? What data will you need?

5 Think about how you will report. No one wants more than headlines, but everyone wants the back-up for the headline statements.

6 Set high targets: 90 per cent impact rather than low targets of 'a majority'. The climate in which the behaviour change occurs is not an immutable given, and L&D can and should influence this climate.[4]

7 Set realistic deadlines for sustained change. What is an acceptable timeframe?

8 Try to quantify what this means to the organization as a whole and for the individual staff going through the learning programme.

9 Hold people accountable for delivering the post-intervention behaviour change. And share the success: it is not an L&D success but the whole organization's. Work with those who get it, and share their practice.

10 Develop excellent practice as it emerges in your organization. Do not have all the answers too early but be very specific about what managers and learners need to do to make that learning high impact.

Notes

1 He quotes Daniel Goodacre III in the first page of Kirkpatrick (1970), saying that 'the philanthropic attitude [to training] has come to be taken for granted'.

2 Jack Phillips established the evaluation method based on ROI (return on investment). His work is developed and sustained through the Jack Phillips ROI Institute.

3 The debate about the primacy of execution over strategy has been critically assessed by Roger Martin in 'The execution trap', *Harvard Business Review,* July 2010.

4 Unpublished research conducted by PWC in its Management Service Practice in Toronto indicated that the 'transfer climate' was a critical factor in the success or failure of learning and development (Jane Botsford, Director of Educational Methods, PwC Management Services LLP).

Performance support

Introduction and context

The clearest definition of performance support is the one given by Gery (1991): 'an orchestrated set of technology-enabled services that provide on-demand access to integrated information, guidance, advice, assistance, training, and tools to enable high-level job performance with a minimum of support from other people'.

There are a number of key phrases in this extract: technology-enabled services, on-demand, integrated information and training, and enabling high-level job performance. If we unpack those, it is clear that what she is talking about is an extension of the concept of on-the-job learning, delivered using technology, at the critical moment of need, and focused on helping the individual perform better and more effectively. In other words, the focus is on helping someone at work at the moment they get 'stuck', and doing so in the most appropriate manner, in the shortest possible time. This is what BP's Nick Shackleton-Jones meant by learning for 'people who care' (see Chapter 3). At that moment of need, the individual is desperate to get an immediate resolution, and highly responsive to learning.

Where performance support distinguishes itself from training is at the point where the services offered extend beyond the parameters of development and spill into information, advice or even a simple checklist. Any one of these options may be, at that moment, more appropriate than a formal learning intervention. The concept of 'on demand' is very important. Performance support is, by definition, at the moment of need. What is supplied at that moment depends on what is needed to resolve the issue, and access to information, guidance, checklists or structured learning have their place depending on what is needed to quickly resolve a specific issue that the individual has encountered at that moment.

Performance support has one simple aim: to improve job performance. The theory is that anyone confronting an immediate job-related problem will work far more effectively if that problem can be solved as close to the moment of need as possible, and in the simplest and least complex and fastest way possible.

The original form of performance support is very familiar. It is enshrined in the old concept of 'sitting next to Nelly'. Almost since the beginning of organized work, somebody who was stuck asked the more knowledgeable person next to him or her to help solve the problem. This is embedded in the even older concept of apprenticeship. If you sat with an expert for a long period of time, and had someone always there to correct your practice, you too, in time, would become an expert. As a worker became more experienced he or she asked fewer questions and began, in turn, to be asked questions by the younger and less experienced members of the workforce. A simple cycle was created for the transmission of knowledge from one generation of the workforce to another, and it is a practice that continues to this day.

What is wrong with this approach? The problem is, the speed of change in the workplace often means that the most knowledgeable person is not necessarily the one who has been there the longest. The complexity of work means that an issue is not necessarily solvable by reference to experience. And the organization of the workplace often means that the person with the answer is no longer sitting next to you but may be in a different building, a different city, or even a different country; if you are working from home, there is no Nelly next door! This is where technology steps in and where performance support takes off.

The pressure of work also means that, often, it is hugely impractical and inefficient for the most experienced person to be taken off the job to answer a basic and perhaps often repeated question, or solve a simple problem. This is not the best use of either their time or their expertise. Imagine that same individual, constantly interrupted, being asked to solve exactly the same issue day after day, week after week and it is easy to see that new models of 'sitting next to Nelly' are required. If you manage to deliver instant performance support without tying up your most experienced staff for most of their working day, you have built something that is more efficient, more up-to-date and more resilient than what went before it.

Not providing that support can be a nightmare! Imagine an individual searching around trying to solve a simple problem, or worse, any number of individuals searching around fruitlessly, attempting in isolation to solve the same problem. There is a massive cost in terms inefficiency, notwithstanding the demotivation this frustration generates. If that frustration is manifested on a regular basis by a large number of individuals for most of their working day, the result will be a very negative, inefficient and ineffective workforce. Many (certainly the best and most able) are very likely to give up in frustration and leave their job.

Performance support is clearly about cutting costs and increasing efficiency by offering the right kind of information or development at the right time in the right way, and getting results in the fastest time possible. It should, therefore, be an obvious choice for improving most organizations, but its modern, technology-based application is relatively poorly adopted. This is because performance support falls between two or three stools: training and development; workplace process development; and organizational efficiency and effectiveness. Given this, the only way performance support will work is if the organization takes a holistic approach to workflow; in other words make big, strategic process decisions that transcend the various functions that own part of this action.

The parallel situation has occurred in the talent management arena. Many companies now appoint someone who has an overview of the whole employee lifecycle and therefore takes strategic decisions about making the process joined up and efficient. This approach embraces recruitment, induction, performance management, career development, promotion and so on.

CASE STUDY   Bob Mosher

To get an expert perspective on performance support, I talked to Bob Mosher. Bob Mosher is the former Senior Director and Learning Evangelist at Microsoft. He left that company in 2006 to join the performance support company Ontuitive. He subsequently left Ontuitive to set up his own company, Apply Synergies, with colleague Dr Conrad Gottfredson.

The summation of his and Gottfredson's work during those first five years became their book, *Innovative Performance Support* (Mosher and Gottfredson, 2011). Mosher embraced the concept of performance support although he had worked for most of his career in a more conventional L&D role. His personal journey reflects a growing impatience with the inadequacies of current L&D practice. The essence of this impatience is in the single solution that L&D applies: a structured learning intervention, as opposed to the more complex analysis of need and the meeting of that need with an appropriate response. This is the model offered by performance support. It does not replace a development strategy: it adds more elements and more effective choices.

More and more large companies are adopting performance support as a core element of their development strategy. Three examples, Herman Miller, McDonald's and Deloitte illustrate the diversity of organization. Each of these companies works in a very different sphere: Herman Miller builds office furniture, McDonald's is probably the world's most famous restaurant chain and Deloitte offers business consultancy and accountancy services. Each of their approaches is very different, but each is fit for purpose and built around the company's needs.

What has allowed performance support to come of age has been the increasing availability of powerful technologies, specifically mobile technologies, that can better enable services that can orchestrate all of the areas that Gery (1991) describes in her definition of performance support given above. Until these technologies were available, performance support was often clunky and clumsy. It did not quite live up to the theoretical expectations that had been elaborated so many years ago. In some ways, the full implementation of performance support has taken over 20 years in gestation to become established and gain traction.

One of the early examples of electronic performance support was provided by the (now defunct) US company Prime Computer (Raybould, 1990). It replaced a large amount of paper information on its products, designed to inform its sales staff, with a (then) state of the art electronic system that provided knowledge when it was needed; at different levels of complexity depending on the enquirer, and which was always current. This had a significant increase in the efficiency of the sales team and resulted in bottom-line improvements.

In many ways this has all the elements of more sophisticated contemporary approaches. Prime used an electronic support mechanism that delivered appropriate information to individuals at the point of need, in a way that had been impossible to deliver hitherto. For the sales staff, being able to make a single enquiry that would deliver the information required was a vast improvement on having to wade through files of paper, some of which would be outdated, to get at the same information. At the point of need, the electronic support system was far more efficient and effective than the paper files and documents that it replaced, in meeting the needs of sales staff. Once the system was established, it was relatively easy to tag new documents and update old ones, so the management of the information was also less complex, faster and more straightforward than reprinting paper documents.

In much the same way, Boeing is replacing its paper flight manuals with electronic content delivered on an iPad. Tests showed that pilots accessing relevant information and checklists under pressure (for example in an emergency) could find the information far quicker using the iPad than accessing the paper manuals. This system has the added advantage of being simple to update. The previous model of sending out new pages with statutory changes, and asking that the old pages be destroyed and replaced, was automated. The new manual is simply downloaded onto the iPad automatically, and Boeing had the reassurance that every manual everywhere in the world is up to date. Instead of a time lag between the issue of an update and its incorporation into the flight manuals, the new method was almost instantaneous. (Conversation with Tom King, Chief Learning Technologist, Boeing Training and Flight Services.)

In addition to iPads, the cockpit of a contemporary passenger aircraft is packed full of performance support. The immediate reaction generated by the plane's computers is backed up by comprehensive information in the flight manuals. The pilot is surrounded by information at his or her fingertips, delivered at the moment of need automatically or on demand.

Performance support is neither a replacement for nor duplication of more conventional training and development. It is always complementary. The overall aim is similar: to build an empowered and self-reliant learner who is independent, self-motivated and able to solve his or her learning needs at the moment those needs manifest themselves, with the minimum of intervention and in the fastest time possible. The difference is that performance support offers a range of solutions up to and including development. The typical L&D response is usually to offer structured learning, or nothing.

Performance support is really the modern, electronic equivalent of having a wise expert at your side who is ready to answer any questions, at any time, so that you can keep working efficiently. This relationship helps build confidence and mastery as the job evolves over time. Knowledge or skills deficits are resolved, sometimes informally, but always far faster than a formal training or development response.

There is a subsidiary issue, in that demand for training and development can create passive learners who expect somebody else to sort out their work-based problems. Performance support drives a culture that provides tools for the individual to resolve his or her own problems at the point when they arise – or at least meets most problems when they arise!

This all fits neatly in with other significant changes occurring in and around workplace learning. It is now no longer plausible, acceptable or desirable to rely on front-loaded skill development, a one-shot solution, which can equip an individual for an entire career. That model has held sway since the Industrial Revolution, but it is completely inadequate to cope with the current working environment. What organizations are trying to establish now is a more dynamic approach to learning that stretches along the entire span of an individual's career. It has to be rapid, efficient, collaborative and self-directed, and increasingly deployed at the moment of need. Performance support has a significant role to play in this environment.

Mosher has defined five critical moments of learning need (Mosher and Gottfredson, 2011):

1 *New:* when learning to do something for the first time.

2 *More:* when expanding the breadth and depth of what has already been learnt.

3 *Apply:* when a learner needs to act on what he or she has learnt. This includes planning, remembering what has been forgotten, or adapting the learning to a specific situation, rather like the role of a help desk.

4 *Solve:* when problems arise or when things break or do not work as intended.

5 *Change:* when people need to learn a new way of doing something to rebuild a skill set that has become deeply ingrained, or develop an entirely new skill set.

Traditional learning provision tends to focus on the first two moments of need only: new to the job, or expanding a role; yet the other three are becoming increasingly important in today's environment and are essential for the growth and development of organizations as well as individuals. The work focus and immediate response to a problem puts performance support at the intersection of work and learning and is becoming an essential component for support doing the job, rather than an add-on or one-off resolution. It keeps the individual working efficiently and can deal with most routine problems. It is clearly not the answer to everything, but it is an important tool in the blended learning toolkit as it addresses core issues at the precise moment of need.

The problem with relying on front-loaded training is that, by definition, it takes the worker off the job, or prevents him or her starting the job, but does not necessarily solve the problems that person will encounter the very next day. It is clear that we need another tool, and performance support meets that need. This is the blended learning model for workplace learning in the new millennium. Mosher's vision is to have both formal and informal learning across the five moments of need. It is an enablement model: you are equipping people with the skills, processes and mental agility to solve their own problems, rather than building a dependence on formal courses or cumbersome, inefficient structures such as staffed help desks.

Performance support develops an ability to sustain work, not just recall previous instruction. The simple analogy, related by Bob Mosher, is that it is like teaching someone how to swim rather than offering them devices that prevent them from drowning. Ultimately the former is preferable to the latter because it builds independence and autonomy.

Every organization has lots of information and resources but the learner can wallow in too much information or poor access to that information. Performance support is about focus: orchestrating solutions in an easily consumable way. If you start with an asset analysis and look at the resources available and work with those, performance support can be relatively simple to orchestrate and implement. Organizations are often further down this road than they realize. What they lack is the infrastructure to implement a worthwhile and robust solution. There may be some L&D organizations digging in their heels and refusing to move forward in this direction, but the trend is abundantly clear. As L&D becomes more strategic and begins to focus on working to achieve the businesses' key performance indicators, it is inevitable that they will move some way down this path.

Most organizations do not bet everything on establishing comprehensive performance support systems and processes. They set it up in a small area to prove the concept, and then move on. For example the office furniture company Herman Miller began that journey when it had a simple Microsoft Office upgrade to implement. It decided not to set up a training programme for staff but established a performance support help system that was dropped right into the application and could be accessed on an 'as needed' online site. Having proved that this model worked, it moved from this to a performance support programme for the launch of a new product. That intervention considerably upped the stakes. Performance support can cover many areas across the whole talent management arena. It is more than programmatic job aids provided for technical support at the time of need. In a similar way to the approach of the L&D manager at Herman Miller, other companies are taking low-risk steps before looking at critical applications.

The focus of performance support is, essentially, on a micro piece of information or learning: enough to solve the problem, but not so much as to hinder the workflow and as a consequence it has had some impact on the rewiring of the concept of a learning object. We often think in far too large blocks; these can sometimes be days or many hours of learning. Performance support is about offering small, focused and targeted amounts of learning at the appropriate moment to solve a specific moment of need. Think minutes not hours.

Getting started involves developing a strategy, then a methodology and then finding the right resources. This integrates well with mainstream L&D, as the first areas often chosen for attention are always ones L&D has had little impact upon. The strategy for introducing performance support requires conversations with at least one line of business. The key question is: what prevents your people achieving X or Y? You look for a small moment of need and then you deal with it. It is a focus on problems that exist now and that can be solved quickly. Because of this, it is often possible for performance support development to go from whiteboard to implementation in six to eight weeks, well below the time needed for developing a piece of dedicated learning material.

The speed of organizational change will require new and more flexible approaches to learning. Learning will be delivered, increasingly, at the point of need and contextually embedded. This will create far more agility in L&D operations. Bob Mosher is sure that organizations have no choice but to move in this direction, as it offers an added dimension to the learning operation and has direct results and payback. Everybody wins. Performance support is not just here to stay, but here to stay as an embedded, coherent and essential part of any kind of staff development strategy.

CASE STUDY   BP

When BP merged with Amoco, the two cultures were wildly divergent. One of the key ways that the companies built a common culture was to set up a core directory of expertise. What this meant, in effect, was a dedicated intranet site, accessible to all staff, that could be searched at any moment of need. It was built around the two companies' core areas of expertise, and indexed by individuals who had that expertise. The resulting product was known as 'Connect'. The right person with the right answer could come from either company, as could the query. Where the enquirer and the owner of the knowledge came from was irrelevant; the issue was: could a problem be dealt with quickly?

The continuous accessing of this database was like a stitching process. Each time someone from BP connected with someone from Amoco, a connection was formed; after thousands of these connections the distinction between the companies began to blur as employees saw themselves as part of one big expert company. This kind of performance support is relatively easy to establish. In this case, a staff member simply needed to access a multiple-use online directory. That timely ability to get hold of an expert improved motivation and performance, without having to set up complex systems or having to tabulate knowledge in a written format. Clearly this is not the answer to all performance support problems, but in this instance it worked well. It was fast to set up, and had the dual function of dealing with real issues and helping staff recognize that they worked better together as one company.

Alison Bickford puts this rather well in a blog she wrote in February 2012. She points out that: 'performance support is about providing staff with access to the right information and people just-in-time at the point of need.' In order that staff can access this information, it has to be placed in the workflow. The best people to decide where and how that information is placed are clearly those working in that department or area. Therefore, the intranet solution that BP used so successfully may not be the one for every circumstance. Simply putting people in touch with each other may not always work either. The key is to consult and listen to the people you are trying to help, and work out what works best for them.

What are the limitations of performance support?

Performance support is not the miraculous answer to all performance issues in an organization. Indeed there have been a number of criticisms of the performance support model; Clark (1992) outlines a number of reservations. The first concerns whether the piecemeal approach of performance support will actually deliver the 'big picture' to users. Learners need a framework on which they build their knowledge. If the small chunks supplied by performance support are 'not explicitly tied to the framework, the learner will not develop the big picture'. By extension, if performance support exists, it may even discourage an individual from fully embracing the training attached to the job, and simply problem solve rather than increase skills and competence.

Performance support rarely puts the learner in control of the learning. In other words, the amount of information supplied is the amount of information supplied! This means that it is difficult to follow up, extend the learning or establish connections between disparate pieces of information. Everything remains fragmented in the support system and, potentially, in the mind of the learner. Clark also worries about how corporate knowledge and collective expertise will increase in that fragmented support environment where everyone has a partial picture.

Clark's final concern is the cost/benefit. Performance support often requires the deployment of complex technology to fix simple problems. And performance support will not work if the support technologies are not kept constantly up to date and monitored for their effectiveness. Panviva, an Australian company, markets a performance support tool called SupportPoint. It interacts with computer systems and supplies immediate help and feedback for the user. This is fairly conventional as performance support systems go; what makes SupportPoint more interesting is that the user can engage with the SupportPoint system at any point. It is possible for the user to supplement the help offered, or correct what is being offered if there is an alternative and better way round the issue. Any changes are flagged up to the support manager who can confirm them or roll back the information to the previous iteration. In some ways, the Panviva example answers some of the criticisms levelled at performance support by Ruth Clark.

It is clear that SupportPoint is attempting to build a body of knowledge alongside the workforce, not independent of the workforce, and it relies on their superior day-to-day knowledge to make the system work at its best. The software works in partnership, complementing the skills and knowledge of the workforce rather than undermining them. This is, undoubtedly, the way that performance support tools will develop in the future as software becomes more intelligent. They will become more interpretive, context sensitive, and behave as active partners with the human beings at the sharp end of the system. In some sense, then, as the performance support tool becomes more effective, the workforce becomes smarter. Everybody wins.

Conclusions

Performance support is an important part of the 'learning on the job' component of workplace development. It does not replace what exists but complements it. How performance support is delivered in an organization will depend on a number of factors and the complexity of the performance support tool will therefore vary greatly. It is clear from the examples described above that not all performance support needs to be complex, expensive and difficult to implement, although in certain areas this may necessarily be the case.

BP gave electronic access to a contact database as a very successful performance support offering. Reuters (now Thomson Reuters) uses SupportPoint to build an interactive add-on to its existing information systems to help staff come to terms with those – often complex – software programs. The brilliance of SupportPoint is that it learns alongside the workforce. The system is not fixed but able to grow organically and, therefore, keep pace with the knowledge and insights offered by the company's best staff. It is not a database of staff expertise as such, but it does embody the expertise of those individuals. In some ways it offers the best of both worlds.

This model is somewhat different from the one employed by Jaguar Land Rover to train its sales staff on the features of new or updated models of its vehicles. Instead of offering information-based software, it has broken the material down into small digestible chunks and allows the sales staff instant access to the information using their iPads. In front of a customer, they can discover the answer to a query and then pass the iPad to the customer to explore more details about the car. All the expertise comes from the team that built the support software together with feedback from the sales staff. Together they helped improve the user interface and speed of access to the material and made it a popular choice to use on the showroom floor.

Just as the 70:20:10 model is gaining widespread acceptance, and learning teams are looking at on-the-job development as well as coaching, feedback, networking and stretch assignments to complement formal learning, performance support is developing into a critical component of this mix. It is not the entire answer, but it complements other forms of development and offers a real benefit to the employee at the moment of need, when support is available quickly and seamlessly. Every learning professional needs to understand performance support and what it can do for their organization.

Ten tips to get you started

1 Look at what other organizations are doing to get an idea of what is possible.

2 Always develop the system with the users in mind and with their active participation.

3 Go for the simplest model possible that will do the job.

4 Start with some area that is low risk before rolling it out more extensively.

5 Quantify the benefits in terms of the problems this will solve.

6 Spend time developing a user interface that is as intuitive as possible.

7 Let the users modify the system and make it better on a continuous basis.

8 Think through what you intend to achieve before you call in experts.

9 Capture the immediate benefits so that you develop a coalition of support.

10 Keep its role in perspective. It does some things well, but not everything.

Instructional design

Introduction

This chapter takes a look at a huge area of investment in corporate learning: instructional design. After examining the history of instructional design, we look at what one of the world's leading experts thinks its role is now. This is contrasted with a broad expert view from the US e-learning guru Elliott Masie. We then look at what four people who work in this area actually do and how their role is evolving.

A brief history of instructional design

In some sense, the history of instructional design can be traced back to 1974 when the first edition of *Principles of Instructional Design* by Gagné and colleagues was first published. Its enduring quality is demonstrated by the fact that it went into a fifth edition in 2004 when new chapters on subjects such as online learning, non-existent in 1974, were added. The book was pioneering because it suggested a consistent and structured process for designing learning experiences that was based on cognitive psychology and information processing theory. It introduced Gagné's famous nine-stage design process, often referred to as the 'nine events of instruction'; this endures to this day.

Robert Gagné was born in 1916 and died in 2002. His best-known book is *Conditions of Learning* (Gagné, 1965), still a seminal text in the field of educational technology. There is a direct link between his 'conditions of learning' and the nine-stage design process; one emerges from the other. Instructional design is a way of building learning events taking account of the optimum conditions that make learning effective. The nine stages[1] are:

1 Gain attention of learners (reception).

2 Inform learners of learning objectives (expectancy).

3 Stimulate recall of prior learning (retrieval).

4 Present the content (stimulus) and break it down into components to avoid information overload (selective perception).

5 Provide learning guidance (semantic encoding).

6 Elicit performance (practice/responding).

7 Provide feedback to learners (reinforcement).

8 Assess their performance (retrieval of information).

9 Enhance knowledge retention and transfer to real-life, authentic work (generalization).

Gagné's nine stages still hold good nearly 40 years after their elaboration, but they also outline the weaknesses of some approaches to instructional design. They encourage an inward focus on the development of learning materials to the exclusion of all else. The model is prescriptive, and therefore ultimately boring, and it is repetitive in a way that makes everything look like everything else. There is little scope for innovation and no attempt to take account of context and learning environment apart from in the final stage of the process. Contemporary figures in the field acknowledge the Gagné legacy but have moved the scope and practice of instructional design a long way from this model.

Some of that trajectory is illustrated in a recent ASTD book by Michael Allen, a well-known United States-based learning developer. His book, *Leaving ADDIE for SAM* (2012) contrasts two very different approaches to learning design. ADDIE is a traditional five-stage model for developing learning materials and stands for Analysis, Design, Development, Implementation and Evaluation (see Figure 7.1); SAM stands for Successive Approximation Model. It was developed and promoted by Florida State University as a robust way of developing learning materials or learning events and expands on the Gagné model by including context. But this too has become overly laborious and slow to implement and more rapid development tools have become more practical and fashionable. Allen's rapid prototyping tool is called SAM. It is a specific model that involves constant iteration of the learning idea using rapid prototyping. It is a much faster and more effective process than the more laborious and time-consuming ADDIE. Its use of computer-based 'outline' and sketching tools has also called time, to a certain extent, on the paper-based and discursive models of old. SAM is not the only

FIGURE 7.1   The ADDIE model

rapid prototyping approach, and ADDIE is not completely redundant, but the trajectory is clear.

A good demonstration of how instructional design has moved forward is to contrast Gagné's nine steps and ADDIE with the more flexible and pragmatic approach that is elaborated by Dr Allison Rossett who was, until recently, the Professor of Educational Technology at San Diego University in the United States. She has written widely on educational technology and instructional design and represents a new approach that resonates more with the wider changes in corporate learning.

CASE STUDY   Professor Allison Rossett

Professor Allison Rossett has authored or co-authored six important books on learning design; the main three are: *Job Aids and Performance Support* (2007), *First Things First* (2009) and *Beyond the Podium* (2001). What links them is Allison's focus on delivering high quality learning and development in an increasingly digital world, and ensuring that non-face-to-face teaching and learning are high quality, student-centred and enjoyable processes. Her view is that there is no excuse for boring learning in whatever context it is delivered.

For Professor Rossett there is a balance between the effort you put into the materials in terms of design and the amount of support you offer the learner directly.

In other words: light on learning, heavy on support works. Heavy on learning, light on support also works. It depends on the context, on the learner and most of all on the learning system that is being constructed. She is, above all, a pragmatist when it comes to instructional design. She does not start with a heavy instructional design model that has to be incorporated into every piece of learning material regardless of context. In many ways, inflexibility is what frustrates people when they encounter old-style instructional design and begin to reject its overtures. In a conversation in September 2013, a head of learning for a major consultancy in the United States told me: 'More and more, I by-pass our instructional design team. They are just too slow and too inflexible when I need speed and pragmatism.'

For Professor Rossett, every piece of learning should thoroughly engage and delight the learner. There is, however, no magic formula that works every time. In her view, the quality that can excite a child using an iPad, for example, has nothing much to do with a lot of online learning, or the drab functional design of many training rooms. Both environments are dull, colourless and boring. What makes them work better is not just changing the layout, but the complete meshing together of form and function, including the use of colour, layout, user legibility and structure. In one sense, this is what she thinks instructional design should be injecting into learning. She is basically a connectivist and a constructivist: she veers away from classic drills, memory work and practice models towards trying to engage people's motivation by offering them scenarios, events to engage with and checklists to analyse their learning, combined with the discovery learning of constructivism. Hers is an instructional design model that aims to touch hearts and minds at the same time.

Professor Rossett defines that model in four ways. The first is building a learning experience that is completely centred on learners in terms of their problems, their tasks and their priorities. Secondly she aims to build learning that is vivid and authentic and which allows the learner both to think and to do something. They need to be engaged to be motivated. Thirdly, the experience has to stretch the learner but also allow some successful steps in that process. Finally, there have to be systematic choices that allow individuals to explore more deeply, extend their learning and take the learning back to the workplace. So this is about challenge, simulation and opportunities to practise coupled with on-demand support. This allows individual learners to take an almost unique path through the material depending on their needs, experience and knowledge.

In Rossett and Sheldon (2001) Professor Rossett suggests eight strategies to engage the hearts and minds of the learner:

1 Ensure that employees experience some success as they grow.

2 Reveal the sources that influence the programme; detail why they are credible to participants; tell people's stories.

3 Used two-sided arguments to make points. Approaches that admit multiple views are more convincing than a one-sided litany.

4 Inoculate learners against future reactions and barriers. Detail ways to handle input and use work-arounds.

5 Use role modelling and role-playing, and include conversations.

6 Use stories, problems, cases and anecdotes. Show emotions and reactions.

7 Encourage reflection about the usefulness and meaning of what is being learnt.

8 Use extrinsic rewards for boring and repetitive tasks.

In many ways, Professor Rossett is putting emotional engagement back into learning. Her view is that successful learning touches both the mind and the heart with stories, case studies and narratives that ring true. Her model is one that offers vivid experiences designed specifically with the end in mind. She wants reflection on what has been learnt, guided choices and rich colour for learning that has the engagement of the learners maintained throughout.

Her view of instructional design is not one of isolated materials that are over-designed and over-elaborate, but of a complete learning system that can include coaching, observation, stretch assignments and the opportunity to practise and gain regular feedback on progress. It is about building successful learning communities and learning structure that goes from a focus on learning to a focus on performance, with constant support. It is instructional design with a finger on the pulse of the organization as well as the learner. It is engaged, practical, pragmatic instructional design, not disengaged or purely theoretical.

This model has been reinforced by my conversations with a number of crucial practitioners in the field. Far from seeing their role as declining, they see it as increasing in scope, complexity and depth. But to do this it has evolved. They all acknowledge that the old models of instructional design are dead or dying and the new role is enduring and powerful.

CASE STUDY   Instructional design vs learning producer

I asked the well-known learning technology expert, Elliott Masie, for his views on the role of instructional design and we discussed the role of an instructional designer. He believes that there are many fewer instructional designers who are full-time employees at major corporations than used to be the case. Some of this role has shifted to suppliers and vendors, and some of the content is being curated, organized and published by people who are defined as content focused, but not trained or tasked as 'instructional designers'. Some organizations want to produce learning and performance content but not in a traditional instructional envelope.

He is moving away from using the title: 'instructional designer' in favour of a more generic title: 'learning producer'. This is because the latter focuses on a wider range of content elements including video, mobile and social/collaborative. That does not undermine staff with learning design and analysis skills, but indicates the shifting roles in corporate learning and a move to broader roles rather than narrow specialisms.

In a more recent blog (Masie, 2013) he talks about 'crowd-sourced learning design'. This new paradigm assumes that a large number of experienced workers in a particular organization would be better placed than a very small number of learning experts to design a new learning activity. This 'wisdom of the crowd' model is a potential design strategy which, again, realigns and questions the role of the specialist instructional designer. He or she needs to shape the ideas from the crowd and work with them to make sense rather than have a carte blanche to do whatever he or she feels is appropriate.

Elliott Masie is by no means unique in his view. Another learning leader told me that she no longer drew upon the expertise of the instructional designers: she had in her own team! 'They tend to slow everything down, complicate the development process, and insist on outmoded paradigms of learning.' So how did we get to this? In the United States at least, most instructional designers have a Master's degree. Those programmes are turning out hundreds of qualified instructional designers every year and yet the very people who should be enthusiastic supporters of rigorous instructional design feel that their approach is outmoded in some way. If the crisis in instructional design has not yet arrived, it is well on its way!

The view from the field

I attempted to explore this area more deeply by talking to a number of practising instructional designers from a wide variety of industries. What is clear from these conversations is that instructional design is on a journey. I will try to describe that journey for you.

I interviewed four people currently working in instructional design across a range of industries in both the United Kingdom and the United States. Much of what they said aligned across all four interviews, but each has a vibrant contribution to make to the learning teams in their various industries and their contributions can neither be ignored nor replaced.

CASE STUDY   Stephanie Dedhar, Learning Designer, BP Online Learning

Stephanie has rebranded herself in a number of ways. She refers to her role as a learning designer rather than instructional designer and has moved in her career from largely focusing on e-learning to a broad and holistic focus on social and informal learning. Her focus is not only about making things look good but also about making them communicate well. Her role is therefore a combination of design and utility. She has come to recognize that visual design works with the design of the user experience. Once, when commissioning materials, she would give graphic designers free rein, but now she takes a much greater interest in the visual side. She offers much more input and is much more demanding about how the visual elements contribute to the quality of the overall user experience.

She is completely comfortable with the growing area of user experience design. She sees this as a critical part of building an effective learning environment overall. Learning resources play a key but not exclusive part in that environment. In other words, the complete user experience is more important than simply focusing on the quality of the resources, and providing learners with alternative pathways through a learning process is crucial in maintaining their interest and engagement and, therefore, in delivering effective learning.

She spends a lot of time working on the words that appear on the screen or the page. In some way she is a translator, moving language from expert input to highly focused communication, without losing meaning. Engagement is extremely important and this requires a focus on detail as well as maintaining a perspective on the overall picture, her audience and the project as a whole; she switches continuously from macro to micro to do her job.

She sees herself as the connection between the subject matter expert and the learner. Often her role is to limit the amount of content the expert wants to include so that the minimum amount necessary to communicate and make the point is used. She is curating other people's content and ensuring that the best is displayed, and that learners do not drown in repetition, duplication and over-complication.

She can add the business context. She makes it her job to know what will work within the parameters of the organizational culture. So when briefing external agencies she becomes, in essence, the mind and spirit of the organization. She supplies the context that an external agency, however talented and creative, cannot provide.

Her role continues to evolve from one of a pure instructional design, ie working largely within Gagné's nine stages of learning design, to one that is broader and more deeply involved with the entire learning context. As new staff come into the company, their expectations and attitudes will mean that the role has to evolve again.

Stephanie has no formal instructional design qualification, but comes to the role with an arts background. She thinks that any kind of creative background working in any kind of creative discipline could adapt to a learning design role. In that sense the traditional instructional design qualification could be a restriction rather than an asset, as it focuses on too narrow a perspective on learning.

Her advice to anyone coming into the field would be to gather together a large number of different perspectives on learning design by engaging with a range of experts through social media. Look at what excites them, examine what their issues may be, and engage with their debates as a participant. It is imperative, in Stephanie's mind, to remain in touch with the shifting sands of corporate learning in order to play the most effective role, rather than apply a fixed and static model to whatever is demanded of you. For example, she is considering the potential role of MOOCs (massive open online courses) in a corporate learning environment at the moment; how could her kind of role add value in this context? Her role is evolving while she remains a key member of her learning team and central to their output.

CASE STUDY   Alison Shea, Associate Director E-Learning, FINRA

Alison Shea's job is, in essence, to craft the learning message so that the learning works. She sees herself as the educational equivalent of a communications manager. She works on messages to ensure that the information supplied delivers the right message as effectively as possible. That includes being clear and concise. But that is not the entire role; it also includes the look and feel of the piece of learning: a combination of language and design. Everything has to align if it is to work successfully; this means she has to have views on all aspects of the learning process.

Her role evolves as technology changes. Once part of her role was to select an appropriate technology from the limited choice available; now there are so many tools and so much technology is in the hands of the learners that she focuses more on building coherent conversations and delivering a coherent message, working with whatever technologies are appropriate.

Increasingly her role is, therefore, facilitative and consultative; she works with the subject matter experts, the technology team, the build team, as well as the learners. She is right in the middle of these groups pulling them together and helping them understand each other's point of view, so that they can work productively and end up with an effective and cost-efficient product. She is the glue that holds the various stakeholders together. It has to be a role that involves working closely with content and with people, which differs from the traditional instructional design role that was wholly focused on the materials as part of the production line.

Because of these large changes, Alison's view is that experience in working with customers and understanding their interests are as vital components of the role as an understanding of learning and teaching. In many ways the design role is one of packaging information so that the learner will 'buy' it. She wants to nurture learners and help the entire team understand how best to meet their needs.

Alison has had every role in learning development. She has built flash content, designed PowerPoint presentations, written learning plans and curricula, consulted in design and built learning structures. All this helps her current role in negotiating with those who build the materials. She knows what is involved, and she knows the language of materials construction, which helps the discussions and negotiations.

She combines both technical skills and learning theory; above all, her role now involves high-level project management skills as she has to bring in projects on time and on budget, working with the respective stakeholders and contractors. She summed this up: 'You need a clear picture of what you are doing and why it is important to the organization, and what the learner needs, plus you need to maintain a focus on getting the detail right.'

She believes that technology will change the role even more. New staff are far more tech savvy than their older counterparts, and they will demand a different kind of learning. She feels that she has to keep up with their skill sets and aspirations and turn them into a development roadmap. Their entry into the workplace could transform classroom training and completely flip online learning.

One of the best tools that she has at her disposal is to engage her learners with great stories. People remember stories far more readily than statements of facts, and they remember them in more detail. The new instructional designer is like the builder of jigsaws. As each jigsaw requires new pieces, these have to be built and each new piece has to be repositioned in the picture in order to fit. The instructional designer has to also decide which of these new pieces to keep, and which to throw out, and which ones are really important and should be given pride of place.

This is a big picture role, thinking about the future of learning and meeting the needs of future employees. It also involves great attention to detail, such as keeping track of which stock photography has been used in a particular resource to avoid repeating it in a new resource. The new instructional designer has a critical role as the eyes and ears of learning, both in terms of representing the learner and in ensuring the overall quality and effectiveness of what is produced.

CASE STUDY Stephanie Moring, Instructional Designer, Thomson Reuters

Stephanie's role is quite simply to turn communication into learning. She works with subject matter experts and others who know the content and are willing to share their knowledge in an explicit way. She has to ensure that what the company produces is structured, engaging, interesting and creates opportunities to learn. She believes that if you want behaviour to change, instructional design is the secret.

The internet has changed her role dramatically. People now have access to knowledge at the moment of need and they no longer have to store knowledge themselves: storing knowledge in your head by memorization or storing it on your hard disk in files and folders are no longer prime ways of recall. The key skill now is knowing where to find something, at that precise moment when you need it. This means that for Stephanie Moring, work is focused increasingly on developing resources for performance support. This means that she is creating resources within the workflow, not separate from it.

To do this effectively, she needs to consult with stakeholders and develop core tools that can facilitate support at the moment of need. Delivering this depends on context. For example, her work could involve organizing an informational website so that it is searchable, or she could be creating a group on a social forum so that learners can easily connect to and learn from each other. This means that the focus is more and more on developing bite-size learning, delivered at the point of need, rather than extended learning resources delivered outside the workflow.

The instructional designer's role is to contribute in-depth knowledge of learning theory to the learning team. Thomson Reuters uses the 4MAT model, which asks what, why, how and what if. All of these elements are important and she is, in essence, the guardian of that structure, ensuring that these key questions are answered. In the case of an online forum, if learners are to use it effectively they need to understand why they are using it, how it works, what it is, and any anomalies they might encounter when they use it. She adds value to the exchange of knowledge by maximizing the uptake and facilitating the process.

It is a role that is constantly engaged with the business on the one hand and the learner on the other, rather than the content itself. She could not do her job without being curious about the content and whether it makes sense: a key part of her role is to put herself in the shoes of the learner. Clicking the 'next' button on 90 slides is never going to be a life enhancing experience, but nor is the experience of someone working his or her way through 90 PowerPoint slides during a two-hour seminar. Her job is to make sure that good content is also good learning, and it can only be good learning if it is both interesting and engaging.

She keeps in touch with a number of external forums and with blogs and networks of other people working in learning design. She feels that there is a rich and generous instructional design community outside her company and it is her job to network in whatever form is appropriate so that she stays in touch, feels contemporary and can get any of her problems debated and solved. She uses the rapid development tool 'Articulate' to develop some of her resources and she is an active member of the Articulate community on the web.

She sums up her role as 'making non-learning professionals understand what learning is'. This means she engages with her community rather than simply developing learning materials. For example, she was given 50 PowerPoint slides to turn into online material. Instead of doing the obvious thing, which would be to put the material into Articulate, she started by trying to understand what was actually required and what the learning was trying to achieve. She worked out that the essence of the task was to make a small change to the process that was already being undertaken by the staff. The result was a one-page document that was extremely effective. She solved the problem by *not* developing learning materials; saying 'no' is a part of her job.

Moring's role is a combination of knowledge and skills about learning, combined with curiosity and the ability to ask really effective questions. None of this would be important if she were unable to influence stakeholders and help them understand what they are trying to achieve and persuade them that their initial analysis of what is required may not be the most effective way forward. She uses a range of relevant tools such as Snaggit, Storyline and Shutterstock alongside her know-how to choose the most effective, appropriate tool and make it work for her. She also has to continuously think differently about her role. For example, she created a board game as a learning experience because it was the most effective way of delivering the learning required. The emphasis is always on effective learning, not on what worked yesterday or stock responses to learning need.

CASE STUDY   Katherine Revel, Practice Leader, Global Programmes for the Centre of Excellence, Leadership and Talent, QBE

Katherine believes that instructional design is the only way to achieve the desired learning outcomes in an organized fashion, and the best way to do this is to embed the desired outcomes in the story. Her role is to work with key staff to facilitate this process. Many of the people she works with have a real appreciation for learning but not a clear understanding of how to make it work effectively.

Katherine is a pragmatist. She does not accept that there are fixed limits to the role of instructional design. She will not be a slave to the 40:1 ratio that is often cited as the amount of time it takes to develop one unit of material. It is a case of talking through the issues, working out what is required and then helping to facilitate the delivery. She feels that instructional design still has an element of mysticism to it. Once upon a time this protected instructional design; now it threatens its very existence. Her role is to design solutions that link to specific business outcomes. She focuses on the need and delivers resources that will meet that need. In her mind, that is the modern role of an instructional designer.

She started in sales training where clarity about outcome is paramount. She knew what was required and designed accordingly. That clear link between learning and business benefit has stayed with her for her entire career. But a business focus does not mean any lesser focus on making learning effective. She encourages designers that she works with to sit in on their own classes. That is the best way to understand what you're putting your learners through!

She is quite hard on herself and sets very high standards. If you know what you are doing in terms of instruction design, if you know your learner and you understand the business, there is no excuse for even a bad pilot let alone a bad programme. Her company eliminated the organizational development role because they saw that learning was able to engage in that process by working through people.

One key role is to explain how staff learn. Once people get this, they come with better ideas and much more realistic expectations about what can be achieved and when. Clarity of understanding about what is needed is incredibly valuable, and she tries to persuade those she works with that you have to get that process down to a fine art before you do anything else. You can then work out a clear strategy in the light of that clarity.

She is currently working on a programme for the top 250 in the company, working with Duke University in Durham, North Carolina. Her job is to codesign the materials and ensure that everything is clear and well received. After helping with the set-up, she focused on the top two tiers to design, deliver and measure. The resulting programme has been delivered on five continents. Designing successful programmes for these audiences requires a thorough understanding of the current state of business and its leaders. There is no reason why a focus on business and good quality learning are mutually exclusive. She works well with subject matter experts to design content, and gets good results by making something tangible out of something that starts off intangible. She can work fast and she is logical, and she can make a good story work well as good learning. She feels these skills are vital but still undervalued. Sometimes that goes for the whole of learning. She would like to see learning taken more seriously by HR. Learning's power to leverage value for the business has been demonstrated, and the value of design and the value-added of instructional design in particular allows that full leverage to occur.

A metaphor for learning design

The Eastern State Penitentiary was the world's first purpose-built prison, operational from 1829 to 1971. It was designed on Benthamite[2] principles by the British architect John de Havilland as a place to inspire penitence (or true regret) in the hearts of the inmates, not just to punish them.

The prison was built on the outskirts of Philadelphia, and incarcerated prisoners from the whole of eastern Pennsylvania. It was built to a strict symmetrical design: it had a rectangular perimeter wall 20 feet high with turrets at the four corners and a castle-like gatehouse entrance in the middle of the front wall. At the centre of the enclosed area was a domed structure and radiating from that area were seven cellblock spokes, rather like the spokes of a wheel stretching out from the hub. Each spoke contained individual cells. Each cell had a skylight and a front and rear entrance.

The cells had running water and a flush toilet (even before the White House was thus equipped). The rear entrance led to a private exercise court-yard with a high wall around it. Prisoners spent their entire sentence in solitary confinement contemplating their crime and, in theory at least, communing with their God. Exercise times were staggered throughout the day so that adjoining cell prisoners were never in the exercise yard at the same time. Prisoners exercised for one hour a day and were locked in their cells for the remaining 23 hours. They were given three hot meals a day. supplied through the front door of their cell., and were visited by their guard once a day. Because of the symmetry of the building, one guard could stand in the dome area and, as he turned slowly round, he could look down each cell block, in turn, to ensure that everything was in order.

The design of the penitentiary was so radical that the architect, De Havilland, was in demand around the world, to build similar establishments; up to 300 were built subsequently. However, this model prison was unsustainable. Very soon after completion, the number of prisoners exceeded the number of cells so that more than one prisoner had to be housed per cell, and then the number of cells was increased by adding new cellblocks and then double and triple height cell blocks. The existing space was built on and guard posts added to the wall's perimeter. Death row blocks and punishment cells below ground were also built. By the time the prison closed in 1971, the place was a complete jumble of mismatched buildings. It was impossible to guard properly and the infrastructure was falling apart. It was almost impossible to discern the original plan, and the whole concept of incarceration and punishment had completely changed. It is now a museum and, amidst the ruins, some of the original structures have been restored.

The lesson of the Eastern State Penitentiary applies neatly to instructional design. It is possible to build the perfect piece of learning using tried and tested instructional design principles. As editing progresses, however, the design is altered and corrupted. If this process continues you end up with such a mess that the original structure is barely discernible, and the whole project fails to function properly. The dilemma is that if you impose a perfect design that does not take account of day-to-day usage, you can end up with something that is unworkable. If you allow that design to be changed again and again, to better fit it to an evolving notion of usage, the original framework fails to operate. The Eastern State Penitentiary is a metaphor for failure at both ends of its history. An over-engineered structure that was designed around a theory that ended up impossible to work in practice led to a chaotic mess, over time, where the overall original design was lost entirely. Five key lessons emerge:

1 Design is not absolute, it is relative. This applies to instructional design as much as to any form of design.

2 Design should lock in with function and not stand alone based on theory.

3 There is a point where the original design ceases to have any value. Try to prevent over-meddling long before chaos ensues.

4 Every design has to be workable in its context.

5 Instructional design is a partnership between content owners and potential learners. It should never stand alone.

Conclusions

Instructional design is at a crossroads. Pursuing complex models and over-elaborate development processes has pushed the need for instructional design to the point of extinction, and isolated instructional designers quietly working away on their brief with little contact with the rest of the business are becoming a thing of the past. The engaged professional working inside the business and interpreting its needs in vivacious and exciting ways is a key element of successful learning development.

Each of the people I interviewed has made a significant contribution to the development of high quality learning in their organization but has not done this by slavishly adhering to inflexible models. They work out what is needed and facilitate conversations between the commissioning body, the end user and the development team. They are the glue that holds learning together.

The problem with this role is that it is not a simple pathway to a job in the way a Master's of instructional design used to be. Each person finds his or her own route and, in many senses, builds their own journey and career. But the key components are an understanding of learning, clear expertise in learning technology, an interest in the business they work in plus an ability to articulate what is required and what it may take to deliver it. They are as interested in building whole learning systems as developing learning materials. They aim to develop excitement and engagement as much as correct structures and processes. It is about a love for developing great learning in all its contrasts rather than a narrow, formal, systems approach to learning. This new approach has a long and rich life ahead of it.

Ten lessons for instructional design

1 Good instructional design is at the heart of learning.

2 Instructional design is now about communication with stakeholders.

3 Instructional design is about interpreting ideas and translating them into learning.

4 There is no longer a fixed model or approach.

5 It is not only materials but whole systems that concern the instructional designer.

6 New technology plays a vital role, but one should not get fixated on one technology.

7 Start with the end in mind, not the design.

8 The user experience is paramount.

9 Learning is becoming more granular; go with that flow.

10 Instructional designers should lobby for their role and skills: there is a critical job to be done and nothing, so far, has replaced those skills or that approach.

Notes

1 Detailed in http://hlwiki.slais.ubc.ca/index.php/Gagne's_Nine_Events_of_Instruction

2 Jeremy Bentham (1748–1842) was a British philosopher and proponent of utilitarianism, a philosophy based on the idea of the greatest good for the greatest number. He was a social reformer.

PART THREE
The Game Changers

Coming to terms with big data and learning analytics

> *Truth is now an algorithm.*
>
> ERIC SCHMIDT, CHAIRMAN, GOOGLE[1]

Context

Five or six years ago it was quite possible to survive, and indeed thrive, as a learning leader supplying only the smallest amount of information about learning success. In fact, success was always judged on numbers. And when I say numbers, I mean the number of people taking courses; the number of people using e-learning; the percentage of places that were filled over the year; and above all on data gathered assiduously from what we somewhat disparagingly call 'happy sheets'.[2]

We always seemed to prove, course after course, and year after year, that 75 per cent of participants either enjoyed or very much enjoyed the learning that was provided for them. If that data was backed by a small increase in the number of staff participating in learning, together with an increase in the percentage of those learners undertaking e-learning, a very nice report could be constructed that would keep everybody happy for another year. Learning volume was increasing, costs were coming down and people liked what was being offered. The mantra was, essentially, that learning was good for organizations. However, you never had to prove why it was good, how it was good, or the ways in which you could have made it better. Learning budgets were often approved with only a cursory scrutiny, until all budgets were under pressure and then the learning budget, as the ultimate 'nice to have', was usually decimated.

Alongside such cursory controls, the ownership of learning was firmly and inexorably tied to the members of the learning team. No one really had much of a stake outside the team apart from staff who, if the learning was not compulsory or compliance-related, quite enjoyed the process and perhaps the break from day-to-day work that it offered. Who can say that this was a bad thing? The problem was, not many people said that it was a particularly good thing or had any idea how the organization benefited from such activity apart from fairly subjective concepts of staff welfare and wellbeing. The fact that learning was a general good became a general truth without much challenge. The mantra was: 'Why not, if we can afford it. And why, if we can't?'

The compulsory elements concerned compliance training, which most users were forced to grit their teeth and complete. Lists of staff who had successfully done this were submitted, to prove that required compliance training had been delivered. In other words, pages had been clicked and multiple-choice tests completed to a minimum standard, as per any legal or regulatory demands. This continued during the decades when organizations, generally, were becoming far more precise about where their resources went and what impact the use of those resources made. As information technology took hold, companies were able to dramatically improve processes and generate far more data about what went on in their company than before. To complement the knowledge, instinct and experience of the senior executive team, data could be used to justify a position (however derived), endorse or undermine a specific strategy, not with hearsay but with tangible evidence. Professional teams were assembled to minutely manage those processes that gathered data and deploy the evidence to executive teams. The results were spectacular: businesses made 2 or 3 per cent efficiency gains year on year and organizations could change tactics very fast.

This kind of agility was celebrated by the CEO of Cisco Systems, John Chambers, who used to proudly claim that Cisco could produce a full profit and loss account at the end of each working day and keep a minute eye on how the business was performing hour by hour. What Cisco achieved more than 15 years ago is now common practice in most large companies. The management writer Charles Handy lamented at one point that we had one chance to use our gains in productivity to make work easier and less demanding, but we chose to take those gains in increased profits and make the process of work harder as a direct result (Handy, 1984).

While this was going on learning had its own technology changes to manage, in particular absorbing the move towards online and the arrival of big complex learning management systems to track learning and build databases of courses. The complex and expensive IT systems that were required, however, continued to focus on gathering the same basic information on completion rates and course access data, alongside other limited data on process rather than impact. L&D staff gathered the same information using technology that had previously been tracked manually. Scope did not alter but efficiency increased.

This began to change around 2005. A new phrase, 'learning analytics' emerged where new and different questions could be asked of learning systems and, to facilitate this, more data on more issues was gathered. At this point, the big consultancies started to get interested. In their eyes human capital was the last great space that was virtually unmeasured. IBM bought Connexia (**http://www.connexiagroup.com**) and Deloitte bought Bersin (**http://home.bersin.com**), both research and learning data companies. The focus was on using data and research to align learning with the business, create better value-for-money options, and therefore use learning directly to continue that process of building more efficient and more effective organizations.

A major new data-driven emphasis began. This was to define the value of the investment in learning by the impact on the business; more specifically the impact on the businesses' key performance indicators. At that point, the message shifted from efficiency of delivery to the effectiveness of the learning. In a speech to the Learning and Performance Institute in London in April 2013, John Mattox, Head of Research at KnowledgeAdvisors, said: 'data starts the conversation about effectiveness'. Data became critical in learning and development as, without it, the important questions were unanswerable.

Why big data now?

The quality guru, W Edwards Deming, is widely attributed with coining the phrase 'In God we trust, all others must bring data.' This phrase lives on in the heart of the huge Indian computer services company, Infosys. The message is displayed in large letters above reception. What Deming did was apply statistical processes to manufacturing industry and gather data at every stage so that those processes could be constantly monitored and improved. All of the ISO quality standards trace their origins back to Deming in some form or other.

Although his impact in the West largely occurred towards the end of his life, from the early 1980s onwards, he had already become a legendary figure in Japan in the decades following World War II. He is largely credited with creating the manufacturing techniques in Japan that made their products (especially cars) a byword for quality and reliability throughout the world. Many of the phrases such as 'Kaizan', or continuous improvement, which have now passed into common language, were built on the Deming 14 principles (see Deming, 1982). He was a pioneer of data-driven decision making in manufacturing at a time when the rapid expansion of demand for consumer products (the 1960s and 70s) had led to lower costs but shocking quality and built-in obsolescence.

He greatly influenced the leaders of huge Japanese companies such as Sony and Toyota. One of his first publications that had an impact in the West was *Some Theory of Sampling* (Deming, 1966). The original 1950 edition caused few waves, but when it was republished in 1966 it achieved much more attention. During that period the attitude towards manufacturing significantly altered; by the time he died in 1993, he had become an iconic agent of change in the rebuilding of industry in the United States, the United Kingdom and elsewhere, even though he had spent half of his life in almost total obscurity. The book gives some indication of his focus, his mathematical and scientific perspective, and his attention to detail. His message at that time went against the general trend. He stated that, if you focused on quality and the total cost of production rather than to trying to build things as cheaply as possible, you would increase productivity and market share. It was only when the US car industry was being undermined by waves of Japanese imports that the Western world sat up and took notice of Deming.

The Harvard Business Review published three separate articles on big data in October 2012. They are introduced with an editorial comment: 'Businesses are collecting more data than they know what to do with. To turn all this information into competitive gold, they'll need new skills and a new management style' (p 13). Or, in the words of Adi Ignatius, the editor of the *Review:* 'Big data is out there. The trick is finding new ways to make it work for you' (p 59) What applies generally to business applies to the L&D function.

In the first article, McAfee and Brynjolfsson trace the competitive advantages that can accrue when big data is captured (2012: 64). They demonstrate how an online bookseller like Amazon exploits its processes to track in great detail customer usage, customer likes and what the customer actually purchases (see Table 8.1). It has far more data than traditional retailers could ever assemble and uses it to build a more accurate and complex picture of its customers' needs and purchasing habits. This is why Amazon suggests items you may like to purchase, and solicits your views so assiduously about what you liked and did not like. In exactly the same way, as learning moves online, there is a huge opportunity to collect similar amounts of data that will yield greater opportunities to make better decisions about what, how and when learning is delivered, in an environment where the technology will help to constantly improve access and delivery systems.

TABLE 8.1 What makes Amazon's business model special?

Amazon	Traditional bookseller
Knows a lot about each customer	Knows virtually nothing
Can track where each customer goes on the site and how long he or she spends looking. Knows the ratio of browse to purchase	Has no idea what the customer looks at, only what he or she purchases
Knows what customers who bought x also purchased then or later	Has almost no ability to track apart from purchases by loyalty card holders
Can target useful information about what is available or what is on sale at each individual	Can only send generic e-mails
Has massive stock choices that are available next day	Can only store limited stock
Can anticipate demand through data analysis and stock accordingly	Any anticipation is mostly guess work
Data heavy	Data light

The *HBR* authors contend that evidence gathered so far suggests that data-driven decisions tend to be better decisions. Companies in the top third of their industry in terms of data-driven decision making were on average 5 per cent more productive and 6 per cent more profitable than their competitors (McAfee and Brynjolfsson, 2012: 64). This means that leaders are able to focus on what is known, rather than what people think about an issue or problem. Data is not there to justify decisions already made, but to actually make decisions directly (p 68). The best way companies can demonstrate that the old order is changing, according to the authors, is for senior executives to allow themselves to be publicly overruled by the data: 'To see data disproving a hunch is a powerful lesson' (p 64).

What drives this is the greater availability of a high volume of data, generated by our connected world and our intelligent machines. The more data that can be cross-referenced the higher the reliability of the conclusions you can draw, and that data comes from a wide variety of sources that include sensors, software and social network comments. The competitive advantage given by the speed of almost real-time decision making leads to increased agility. The old model of using structured databases to store one kind of information is clearly too slow and too inflexible to compete; the key is multiple sources of data woven into insights. This is a new field requiring new kinds of expertise.

Why learning analytics?

None of Deming's principles has really been challenged in the years since his death. Indeed, the general high quality of manufactured goods around the world still owes much to his philosophy and focus on quality improvement driven by data. Customers expect good design, reliability and longevity, and generally get it.

For many years now, most organizations have been run on data-based processes. Our ability to know precisely what things cost, how long they took to manufacture and how efficient those processes are has long been taken for granted amongst volume manufacturers. It is no surprise, then, that the attention of organizations has switched to the efficiency and effectiveness of their investment in human capital and within that frame a focus specifically on learning. This is partly because it is an expensive investment and partly because there is more available, but mostly because effectively targeted learning makes a huge difference to overall organization performance.

Investment in learning adds to the cost of employing staff. Good companies spend around 4 per cent of their gross salary budget on L&D; high-tech companies tend to spend a lot more (CIPD, 2012). To leverage this investment and to get more business impact from it makes a lot of sense. That is why big data is beginning to make an impact in learning and we have a new breed of learning professionals being recruited to orchestrate and manage learning analytics:

1 With more complex software running things, more data emerges as a by-product. This data can be analysed with cheap tools and the results fed into strategic analysis and development.

2 As stated above, the big consultancies see human capital as the last space that remains the least measured. They are now developing smart services to remedy that and to help organizations gain efficiencies in their human capital deployment. Learning is an important part of that process.

3 Employers want to know how they can align more closely their investment L&D with the needs of their business. As companies feel the pressure of change and the demands of a fast-paced global economy, they need the L&D operations to deliver the goods and ultimately survive. In a knowledge economy, how you manage and develop knowledge becomes increasingly important.

It is clear that the front-loaded model of training has given way to a process of continuous learning and continuous updating. Early career loading is inadequate when organizations have to move quickly to adapt to changing circumstances. It is also clear that relying only on formal courses delivered at great expense, and accessible only occasionally, will not keep pace with changing demands. The need to update and share knowledge, develop new skills and competences on a regular basis is increasingly self-evident. Big data did not reveal this, but can be a significant factor in making the process of realignment much easier by pinpointing need faster.

CASE STUDY Google

In 2009 the search company Google was aware of its poor leadership that was resulting in talented staff leaving and many highly skilled engineers performing sub-optimally. Conventional leadership programmes were having limited impact, so Google used data to pinpoint what was needed in terms of leadership development. It targeted the performance data it had gathered over many years and sifted it to see what insights emerged. This became known as Project Oxygen.

Massive amounts of data existed on appraisal, performance interviews, successful and unsuccessful leadership in the organization and other reviews and reports that were directly related, but it had never been collated or analysed. Project Oxygen made sure all the data was collected, tabulated and analysed. From that analysis, eight key traits of successful leadership emerged. Good managers were good coaches; they empowered their teams and did not micromanage. They also expressed an interest in and concern for the team's success and wellbeing, were productive and results-oriented, were both good listeners and sharers of information. They helped their team's career development, and had a good vision and strategy for their team. Finally, the good leader had important technical skills that helped the manager develop the team professionally. The very best leaders in Google demonstrated those traits; the poorer leaders did not.

As a consequence of this data analysis, the old leadership programmes were discontinued and new leadership development programmes were built around reinforcing and developing those eight traits. The focus was to raise the overall standard of leadership by concentrating on the quality of leadership of the poorest performing 25 per cent. This strategy was remarkably effective. (Emma Rappaport, conference presentation, April 2014, London)

Google processed large amounts of data that lay relatively untouched on its servers to work out a targeted and focused solution to a specific problem, which would have ramifications across the whole company. In this instance, Google used its own data to start conversations about the effectiveness of its leaders and realigned its development spend on leadership to target what the business needed. The whole process was data driven. This is learning analytics in action.

Using learning analytics

Calling something 'big data' is not really an indicator of quantity; it is an indicator of complexity. For some organizations gigabytes of data will trigger the need to review data management processes; for others it could be terabytes of data that create the need to review the processing, analysis and reporting. The data that emerges from increasingly ubiquitous sensing devices, mobile devices and software logs, can be coupled with wireless data and other information generated by 'the internet of things', as well as data generated by our 'always on' society. Conventional databases cannot handle this data or make sense of it properly. The key is not being able to track single sources of data but rather to weave those sources into a complex data stream that yields meaning.

This is nothing new; companies like Walmart in the United States have been data-driven for years and have reaped the profits from deeply embedding those processes into the way the company operates (Birst, 2012). Raine and Wellman (2012) categorize big data as:

> a loosely defined term used to describe datasets so large and complex they become awkward to work with using standard statistical software. The rise of digital and mobile communications has made the world become more connected, networked and traceable and has typically led to the availability of such large-scale datasets.

Learning analytics emerges from the generic opportunities that big data offers. The Athabasca academic, George Siemens, reminds us that 'learning analytics is hardly new. It has roots in various fields, including business intelligence, HCI, assessment/evaluation, and research models in general' (Siemens, 2011). But there are striking new elements that make learning analytics today different from previous iterations. The key issue is, in George Siemens words: 'the rise of the quantity and quality of data being captured as learners engage in the learning process'. He identifies three separate strands of big data in learning:

1 *Educational data mining*, which is the gathering of information from multiple sources for the explicit purpose of understanding and improving educational processes.

2 *Learning analytics*, which is 'the measurement, collection, analysis and reporting of data about learners and their contexts, for purposes of understanding and optimizing learning and the environments in which it occurs'(p 34).

3 *Academic analytics*; in contrast, this is defined as 'the application of business intelligence in education and emphasizes analytics at institutional, regional, and international levels' (Norris *et al*, 2003: 26).

Siemens and Long (2011) make the simple point that 'basing decisions on data and evidence seems stunningly obvious'. Yet confusion about what that process entails and the slow speed of analysis in traditional learning institutions have made the area less straightforward than it might have been.

Learning analytics allows us to understand more clearly where and why learning is successful and therefore begin to optimize the learning environment to ensure that it delivers better value for money and a bigger business impact.

It can therefore help us rationalize provision, examine its wider impact across the whole organization and help us pinpoint the areas where intervention is necessary.

One huge advantage is that the data is generated in a continuous stream and we can intervene whenever necessary rather than wait until the end of the process to gather summative data and then go back and revise. By definition this is a holistic process that gets at the impact on the organization as a whole and beyond the merely pedagogical or technical. It helps us reveal the scaffolding that underpins any learning system and thereby helps us build or improve systems at a fundamental level. Competitive advantage clearly accrues from being early into these processes.

Birst (2012) identifies three related requirements that precede going down the big data route. The first is storage and the management of the data stored. This whole area has been revolutionized by the access to cloud-based technologies. What was once expensive to purchase and complex to manage now becomes simple and straightforward. The key is recruiting high-quality staff to manage the input and output. The second core requirement is 'mapping and understanding', ie complete 'solutions' or tools that manage the analysis and interpretation of the data. The third involves building analytic processes and integrating them into the workflow so that you can act on the data lessons as fast as possible.

The practicalities of learning analytics

Norris *et al* (2003) suggested viewing knowledge through a number of different lenses: know what, know who, know how, know why, know where, know when and know if. The separation of these focus areas translates quite conveniently into what we might want to know about a learning programme, for example, and analytics can provide us with many of the answers.

We need to know what the programme covers down to a fairly granular level so we can ascertain which bits work and which bits do not. We need to know who has taken the programme, what networks they belong to and what they have been saying about the programme. We need to know how they learnt, and their degree of engagement with the programme. We need to know why they took this programme and the working context that led to that decision. We need to know where they learnt and their mode of learning, and we need to know the precise times when they were engaged and, if possible, the depth of engagement. Finally, we need to understand how much of the learning met their needs, helped them in a specific work-based problem or equipped them to deal with contingencies they have yet to meet but could encounter in the future.

It is impossible to gather all this data manually. A researcher with a clipboard would need to shadow each individual learner to monitor what they did, when they did it, and with whom. This is totally impractical, but we now have technologies that can provide data on all these points of query, and if that data can be gathered on a large scale we begin to get a significant impact assessment of how a specific programme worked and what effect it made on overall business performance.

Some of this data is already routinely gathered, such as log-on information, but not used as part of the analysis. Some information will have to be collected from scratch and therefore systems will need to be set up to collect this data. Clearly there will come a point where the effort involved in collecting the data is simply too great for the value of the data collected, so pragmatism is important. But it is obvious that, when you know a lot more about the detailed processes involved in learning, you are able to make far more informed conclusions about its effectiveness and impact. Essentially, what you are doing is turning a random stream of data related to learning into actionable business intelligence.

What you need, therefore, are established and consistent processes together with standards for data collection and some way of assessing data integrity. Then you need a means of feeding this data into some kind of analytics engine. Over and above the mechanics of delivery and analysis, however, is the need for a strong culture where there is a real commitment to acting on the conclusions, and strong leadership to make sure that the processes have integrity, credibility and buy-in.

A simple model

A simple model that is used by KnowledgeAdvisors looks at input, activities, outputs, outcomes and impacts. In other words, the model looks at what has been invested in the product, what actually takes place, and what happens as a result. If you take this evidence, you can work out the ultimate impact on the business.

It is impossible to completely isolate the impact of training from all the other variables in an organization. The cost of doing this would be too high, and probably unnecessary, but it is possible to carry out the same data gathering for two separate groups, one that has gone through the process and another that has not. This will give you your 'roughly reasonable data' that

KnowledgeAdvisors suggests you should aim for – not perfect data with guaranteed conclusions, but roughly reasonable data with defendable conclusions. There is a balance between cost and certainty that every organization working in this field needs to define for itself.

If what we are looking at is, for example, a leadership programme, we need to ask the managers and perhaps the peers of the prospective learners what sort of changes in behaviour will be expected as a result of the programme. By extension, it is also possible to begin to score where the individual is currently on a scale of, say, 1 to 10 and where it would be desirable for that individual to end up if the programme is successful. You can average this out for the entire cohort.

After the programme has run, you can ask the same questions 30 or 60 days later and get another score that can be correlated with the self-analysis of the participants. This will give you an indication of the impact that the programme has achieved. So, if before the course the average scores were 4 and after the programme they had risen to 6, you have some hard data on impact and effectiveness.

Some of these performance elements can be turned into time saving and/or direct cost saving, so you can end up with some rough data. For example, if the average time saving generated by the programme is the equivalent of one morning a week, this means that there is an approximate saving of 10 per cent of the salary bill. If the average time saving is 6 per cent and the total cost of employing the cohort is £2 million, the saving works out at £120,000. If the programme cost £50,000 to run (including the cost of the participants being off-task) it is easy to work out the net gain. To this calculation you should add qualitative data such as feelings of being more effective, wellbeing and greater team effectiveness. From the combination of all this data you get a broad overview of the degree of success the programme achieved.

If you are gathering more sophisticated data you can look at the areas that are most effective, the delivery methods that work best, the impact of mentoring and coaching, the need for further line manager support, the impact of preparation before, feedback after the event and so on. All of these factors begin to paint a fuller and fuller picture.

If your measurements and data show there is no discernible improvement after 60 days then the programme has been ineffective in spite of the fact that the participants enjoyed it or found it stimulating. It is possible, using data, to take a dispassionate and pragmatic view of impact and establish a way of building in continuous improvement to a programme, while maintaining its alignment with business needs. It is hard to imagine, using this model, how a programme that delivers measurable return could be seen as irrelevant or simply 'nice to have' rather than critical.

The measure of effort that is put into gathering data, however, should be in proportion to the importance of the activity. You do not need to get obsessed with crude measures of return on investment (ROI), but rather build a more complex assessment of your return on talent (ROT): what you have invested in an individual or in a group, how they have responded to that investment and what they have delivered back into the company. Ultimately what you need are stable data-gathering systems to produce a simple dashboard that updates automatically and gives you a chance to monitor, constantly, the impact of what you are delivering and to drill down deeper when necessary.

If your data points can be matched against similar data points from other organizations, there is the opportunity to benchmark what you do against some kind of norm for your industry or sector. This will allow you to see if your investment is at the optimum, and if it is not you should have some clear indicators about how you can move it towards that point.

With an increased focus on learning analytics there is a genuine shift in attitudes about learning. It is seen as one of the processes in an organization that can be monitored, measured and constantly improved. Whenever you introduce something new, you should be thinking about how you incorporate its outcomes into your impact assessment. When you review your learning you are reviewing the direct impact on the business expressed as honestly as possible, using cost-effective tools at the optimum point between reliability and cost. Delivering this will be an enormous challenge, but as necessary as it is desirable.

Implementing learning analytics

If you want to implement learning analytics here are eight things to consider:

1 Ask good questions. Even simple questions that you ask of the learner can be effective. For example, it is much more useful to ask a learner: 'Would you recommend this programme to others' than, 'Did you enjoy this course'.

2 The big aim behind big data is to make better decisions and increase learning alignment. Spreadsheets with data are no more than starting points. The best learning leaders use that data to tell a story and to draw conclusions.

3 The best conclusions, and the most successful presentations, are brief. Tell your story, state your conclusion and what you propose to do and leave the data to back up your argument. Do not drown your audience in data simply because it exists.

4 It is impossible and very costly to measure everything. Pick what is most important and get good data. Some programmes will need only a cursory examination while others will need a more in-depth analysis. You begin with a question that you want an answer to; you do not begin with gathering data to see where it may lead.

5 Always bear in mind that, in most cases, 'roughly reasonable data' is perfectly acceptable provided you are honest about its status and the level of doubt that remains. The cost and complexity of being certain is usually unacceptable; you are trying to improve learning in your organization, not introduce a new medicine to market!

6 The impact of any kind of learning programme can only be ascertained one or two months after the event. What you want to indicate is whether behaviour has changed and skills have become embedded. Gathering data about this the day after a programme is far less compelling.

7 You don't have to be an expert in statistics to tell the right story. If the data is complex someone can help you make sense of it, but you should own the conclusions and be comfortable with explaining them. You need roughly reasonable data that indicates pretty accurately the direction of travel. The more you get caught up in the data the more convoluted and incomprehensible your story will become.

8 Use tools. There are many companies that can help process data and visualize the conclusions, helping to simplify the process.

Conclusions: the bigger picture

According to George Siemens, quoted earlier, learning analytics offers evaluation opportunities that more limited data collection models simply cannot. He claims that most systems are, by their nature, reductionist; in other words, they tend to focus on what you can count rather than take a more holistic approach that goes beyond the components. This is what learning analytics encourages, at least in theory. Learning analytics should also allow for measuring impact in context rather than in isolation. By doing this it can get at some of the social and technical issues, not just the pedagogy.

The essential message is that this is the way to approach those topics and issues that are of interest beyond the learning function. If you can get the model right, you begin to have far more challenging conversations with the rest of the business.

There are many ways that you can begin to collect data. For example, you can look at the way in which learning content is used, in as much detail as you need, together with analytics that can examine different modes of learning, comparing the impact of digital and face-to-face learning. This is on top of the data that the learning system will generate for you. Critically it will also allow you to gather data on the effectiveness of various kinds of intervention: you can bring together the elements of learning that concern dialogue, individual study, support and technological infrastructure. This will allow you to take a view on impact and effectiveness at a macro level as well as those aspects that are most successful at a micro level.

Where to start

1 Work out the questions you are trying to answer *first*.

2 See what data you already have from learning and around the organization and what you need to collect from scratch.

3 Work out how you can process this data quickly and regularly.

4 Define how you will present the conclusions and what you will present to whom. Not all data fits every need.

5 Think about the micro needs (modifying the programme to make it more effective) and the macro needs (how the strategy will be altered in light of these findings). Consider what you have to do in the longer term.

6 Just start!

The final image to leave you with comes from those articles in the *Harvard Business Review* (McAfee and Brynjolfsson, 2012), on the role of data scientists who will be at the heart of this development. The authors urge us to think of big data 'as an epic wave gathering now, starting to crest. If you want to catch it, you need people who can surf' (p 76). This applies equally to learning data as to any other kind.

Notes

1   Comment on 'Start the Week', BBC Radio 4, 27 May 2013

2   A term used for multiple choice evaluation sheets given out at the end of a course, covering content, accommodations, presenter, etc ranked on a scale from completely unsatisfied to completely satisfied.

The lessons from neuroscience

Setting the scene

The vast majority of knowledge about how the brain works has been acquired in the last 20 or 30 years. This does not mean that brilliant (and mostly theoretical) work was not done in the 20th century, but more fundamental information about the brain is now becoming available. Key to this has been our ability to exploit technologies that allow us to witness the brain at work. MRI and PET scans probe deep into the brain and can monitor changes in function and the reaction of the brain to different kinds of stimulation, and record the outcomes. This has supplanted surmise with actual data and we are learning much more about one of the most important functions of the brain: how it learns and when we learn most effectively. The conclusions are beginning to stack up. The 2011 Royal Society Report[1] lists five things that aid effective learning:

1 Emotional engagement with what is being learnt.

2 Keeping up physical exercise to prepare the brain for learning as well as maintaining learning energy.

3 We learn better in stimulating environments, both online and physically.

4 The aging brain needs special attention but can maintain learning throughout life.

5 The brain needs time to reflect to embed the learning.

Professor Guy Claxton, the British author and academic, claims that:

> learning is a subtle multifaceted craft that people can get better at, and it depends on habits of mind not just data, reasoning, decisiveness and training. The brain needs key learning habits like inquisitiveness, perceptiveness,

determination and scepticism and expansive environments cultivate these.

So managers (at work) need to be coaches of learning power. (Claxton, 2014)

Caine and Caine (1994) define three conditions for learning: relaxed alertness, consisting of low threat and high challenge; immersion of the learner in multiple, complex, authentic experiences; and active processing to make meaning.

These conclusions overlap and indicate how effective learning can be engineered with some precision. Up until recently the only way we could work out what was going on in the brain was to measure external stimuli such as pulse rate or electrical activity, or study brain injury to see what impact that had on brain function. Most of what we knew about the internal structure of the brain we learnt by dissection and this meant, obviously, a dead brain. For example, we still refer to the brain as 'grey matter'; indeed a brain that has been preserved in formaldehyde looks grey. The reality though is that the living brain is grey, white and black with a large amount of red and pink due to the blood flow running through it.

Over time, through some observation and guesswork, we built up an image of the brain and how it works that is almost entirely false, and virtually all our teachers and learning professionals grew up and were trained in an era that perpetuated this inaccurate information. The starkest of these myths was the belief that, once part of the brain was damaged, the area that was controlled by that section of the brain could never be made to function properly again, and as we got older it became harder to learn anything new as the brain gradually became 'fixed' and inflexible. For example, we know that Broca's area (a small area at the front left side of the brain defined as Brodmann's area 44 and 45), controls speech. This was discovered by the French physician Pierre Paul Broca in 1861 when he examined the brains of two of his patients who had lost the power of speech and discovered lesions in the same part of the frontal lobe of their brain. If this area was damaged by a stroke, for example, the individual lost the power of speech. However, we now know that if this area is slowly and progressively damaged by, say a brain tumour, the brain manages to retain the ability to generate speech. This suggests that the speech function can transfer to nearby parts of the brain to compensate for the loss at the original site (Plaza *et al*, 2009).

This is a demonstration of one of the most significant discoveries of the last 30 years: the continuing plasticity of the brain. The brain can remake itself throughout life, and it can modify itself to the point where some functions that were deemed no longer available can, with the right exercises and practice, be recovered. This has massive implications for brain damage and aging, to the point where Dr Joel Kramer of the San Francisco Osher Center for Integrative Medicine can, with confidence, make this radical claim: 'Aging can have a significant impact on brain structure and function, but these changes are neither universal nor inevitable' (UCTV lecture on memory and aging).

Brain development

If you want further proof, there is no better indication of the brain's plasticity than *The Woman who Changed Her Brain* (Arrowsmith-Young, 2012). Arrowsmith-Young was born with severe learning disabilities. She developed a number of brain training exercises that allowed her to systematically overcome her neurological deficits. She did this in the face of ridicule by psychologists and doctors and her persistence, inspired by the Russian psychologist Aleksandr Luria (1902–77), paid off spectacularly.

Luria was a pioneer neuropsychologist who worked on the links between language, thought and cortical function. He particularly focused on the ability of the brain to compensate for poor functionality, and it was this aspect of his work that helped Arrowsmith-Young develop her own compensatory methodology. So convinced was she of the efficacy of her technique that she established a number of dedicated schools that teach her work, extend her research and offer help to people with a number of designated cognitive disabilities. The Arrowsmith Cognitive Training Programme was begun by her in Toronto in 1978 and is now used in schools right across North America.

The level of her disabilities was severe. She could not process concepts or read well. She wrote everything backwards, got lost on the street all the time, even close to her home, and was completely physically uncoordinated. Everything she did and everything she achieved over time was due to the neuroplasticity of her own brain. By tailoring exercises to compensate for cognitive deficits, she overcame her disabilities one by one. Even when she had proved what could be done to alleviate the symptoms and overcome the disabilities associated with cognitive deficits, many in the medical and psychological professions refused to believe that what she achieved was possible. The course of her journey from the 1970s to the 2010s is one of gradual, systematic acceptance that her view of the world, and her view of the brain, is correct. Her opponents' views on the brain's limitations were simply inadequate and based on faulty data and inadequate research:

> In 1977, when I began exploring neuroplasticity, it was terra incognita –
> certainly in education. Now it is undisputed that the brain is plastic, malleable

and capable of change. This is the biggest discovery about the brain in
the past 400 years, lifting it out of what Norman Doidge calls 'the dark ages
of neuroplasticity' and overturning centuries of conventional wisdom that
the structure of the brain could not be modified. (Arrowsmith-Young, 2012)

Arrowsmith-Young's work focused on repairing the neural network in the
brain. She proved that neurons respond to stimulation and, when neurons
fire, they wire or link to other neurons, so 'networks of neurons are set up to
perform particular functions: process information, form and retain memories,
navigating space, recognize familiar faces, and parse speech'. Her other discovery was that complex, behavioural processes are not localized (as had been
previously thought) but distributed in the brain, and the contribution of 'each
cortical zone to the entire functional system [or neural network] is very specific'
(Arrowsmith-Young, 2012, quoting Russian psychologist Luria).

Arrowsmith-Young did not discover the concept that 'cells that fire together
wire together' but she exploited its logic. The phrase was coined, in fact, by
Donald Hebb (1904–85) and is known as Hebb's Rule, first outlined in his
most famous book, *The Organisation of Behaviour: A neuropsychological
theory*, published in 1949. As with many neurological breakthroughs, Hebb's
work was entirely theoretical and not accepted at the time of publication.
Gradually it came into prominence after his death. Raymond Klein, in a
tribute to the work of Hebb, claimed in 1999 that:

His view of psychology as a biological science and his neuropsychological
cell-assembly proposal rejuvenated interest in physiological psychology.
Since his death, Hebb's seminal ideas exert an ever-growing influence on
those interested in mind (cognitive science), brain (neuroscience), and
how brains implement mind (cognitive neuroscience). (Klein, 1999)

Arrowsmith-Young's reading led her to surmise that when one area of the
brain was weaker in functioning, learning activities were impaired, and
because of the linkage across the brain, it followed that weakness in one area
could have a wide-reaching impact on many aspects of learning. She decided
to investigate the theories by using her own brain as the test bed. This led
her to develop cognitive exercises for her own deficit areas, this long before
brain imaging allowed scientists to pinpoint such weaknesses in the brain.

Her exercises – which were first used on herself and then extended to
others – simply forced the brain to use those areas that were weak. Through
repeated exercises, cognitive abilities and processes were improved in those
targeted areas, with improved learning capacity the direct consequence. What
had started out as her (theoretical) intuitive understanding was gradually
proved by scientific experiment to be accurate. What she demonstrated was

that by consciously placing demands on certain areas of the brain over a sustained period, the brain actually changed. This change was not temporary but permanent. The analogy is of a wiring circuit board. It may be difficult and fiddly to get the wires in place to create the circuits, but once they are there, they remain there and remain functioning.

One myth about the brain that she challenged was the widely held view that the brain is like a muscle. Using that analogy, the brain would get stronger if you exercised it, and it would revert to the weaker state once the exercises stopped. Her research proved that this was untrue: her links were permanent once the neural network had been established. She says at the end of her book:

> My vision is for all schools to become places where children can go to strengthen their brains so they can learn effectively and efficiently. Cognitive exercises, using the principles of neuroplasticity, will become an integral part of each school's curriculum. In this way, learning problems can be addressed early, as part of a regular curriculum, and students without cognitive deficits will all benefit from cognitive stimulation. (Arrowsmith-Young, 2012)

Contemporary neuroscientists have picked up and extended Hebb's legacy and in so doing have confirmed Arrowsmith-Young's findings. One of the most respected neuroscientists and an expert on brain plasticity is Michael Merzenich, Professor of Neuroscience at the University of California San Francisco. His belief is that humans can continue to modify their brain throughout life:

> Now that science is telling us that you are in charge, that it's under your control, that your happiness, your wellbeing, your abilities, your capacities, are capable of continuous modification, continuous improvement, and you're the responsible agent and party. Of course a lot of people will ignore this advice. It will be a long time before they really understand it. (Merzenich, 2009)

This is substantiated by research carried out at the University of California at San Francisco Osher Center for Integrative Medicine. Dr Joel Kramer and his team examined the brains of older adults for signs of Alzheimer's disease. They discovered that two adults with equally clear indications of the amyloid plaques that are strong indicators of Alzheimer's disease behaved completely differently. One showed clear symptoms of the disease while the other person behaved normally. Kramer came up with the phrase 'cognitive reserve' to explain this: those who continue to develop their cognitive functions through-out life and particularly in their 50s build a cognitive reserve that allows their brains to cope with impairments and pathological changes. It is worth repeating his claim that: 'Aging can have a significant impact on brain structure and function, but these changes are neither universal nor inevitable' (Kramer, 2012). This is a remarkable statement, but his Osher Center research indicates that cognitive reserve can be built by good diet, physical and cognitive and social activity, good sleep and minimizing inflammation and physical pain. Genetic factors are obviously significant but not in terms of outcome. That is why he advises his patients to keep their neurons happy as they can serve someone for a lifetime!

What we know about the brain and the lessons for learning

The implications of neuroscience research on teaching and learning have been widely publicized for well over 10 years. A report by Dr Sarah-Jayne Blakemore and Dr Uta Frith, first published in April 2001, ends with a plea:

> With more active discussion and collaboration between neuroscientists and educators, there is potential for totally new questions to emerge that so far could not be answered and hence were never asked. Such an approach will help to stimulate new research in an interdisciplinary science of learning. (Blakemore and Frith, 2001)

The report tracks recent neuroscientific research on 'how the adult brain learns new material, how learning is affected by emotion, context and individual learning differences'. The nature of learning throughout life is the focus of the second section of the report; the third part addresses individual differences and learning problems. Throughout, the report asks questions and makes suggestions for future interdisciplinary study on neuroscience and learning. Much of what Blakemore and Frith requested at the beginning of the century is bearing real fruit in its second decade. One step forward in this area was the launch of the *Brain, Mind and Education Journal* in 2007, and the publication of the Royal Society report on neuroscience and education in 2011.

A recent book by Dr Paul Howard-Jones (2010) attempts to do exactly what Blakemore and Frith requested, ie forge a new language that is common to both neuroscientists and educators. He calls this new area 'neuroeducational research'. He explains the excitement that it is generating but also cautions against drawing too rapid a conclusion or perpetrating what he calls 'neuro-myths'. We are still operating in a field that is rapidly developing and too rapidly-drawn conclusions could be disproved tomorrow. However, there is still much that can be taken from the current research that can enrich the process of adult learning and make the practice of development more efficient and more effective. He explains:

> Learning is chiefly associated less with the birth of neurons and more with 'synaptic plasticity' – changes in the connectivity between neurons. These changes appear to occur in waves. After birth there is a massive increase in synaptogenesis, ie there is a huge blossoming of connections, such that an infant brain is more connected than an adult's. Then follows a wave of synaptic pruning, in which connections are cut back as the brain adapts to the direct stimulations in its environment. These changes occur at different rates in different parts of the brain. (Howard-Jones, 2010)

Current research has spawned a revival of genetic determinism – we are limited by our genetic make up to a significant extent in terms of learning achievement – but Howard-Jones disputes this: 'so even at the level of gene activity, interaction with experience and the environment is likely to play a crucial role in normal brain development (Howard-Jones, 2010). Critically, Howard-Jones and others attest that the brain's continued plasticity means that it is well-suited for lifelong learning and it has an uncanny ability to adapt to new situations and experiences. What Barbara Arrowsmith-Young grasped by intuition and trial and error, scientists can now prove: learning can alter the structure of the brain. It is also becoming clearer that maintaining intellectual challenge throughout life reduces the chances of developing the symptoms of Alzheimer's and dementia. Other research conclusions reinforce the notion of continuing plasticity, including 'compensatory changes in brain functionality' (Howard-Jones, 2010) as the brain ages. There is also increasing evidence of the positive effect of exercise on the aging brain's capacity to learn, as exercise increases blood flow to the brain.

Other research has demonstrated that multimodal stimulus of the brain produces more activity than each mode generates separately. In other words, providing multimedia learning resources improves cognition and learning effectiveness (Howard-Jones, 2010, referring to research by Beauchamp and Kennewell, 2004). We also now know that visualization is a powerful way of engaging the brain: mental imagery engages almost as much of the brain as the actual experience or object would. This makes a powerful case for practice and simulation in learning to reinforce behaviour change. It is already widely used in sport (as visualization techniques) to prepare athletes for peak performance.

The publication by the Royal Society of *Neuroscience: Implications for education and lifelong learning* in February 2011 was a vindication of the importance of this new field. The committee that produced the report was a Who's Who of British neuroscience; it was chaired by Dr Uta Frith and included her colleague Dr Sarah Jayne Blakemore, both of whom produced the earlier report cited above. It also included Dr Paul Howard-Jones, Professor Colin Blakemore from Oxford University, and Professor Eleanor Maguire from University College London, who produced the definitive research on how London taxi drivers' brains develop through their study of 'The knowledge'.

'The knowledge' is shorthand for learning every road in London. Every London taxi driver has to go through a test of that knowledge before he or she is awarded a licence. The learning process takes about three years. Trainees drive around the streets, memorizing vast amounts of cartographic data. Any London taxi driver can visualize a route from any one point to any other in London, and can describe each road, turn, traffic light or round-about between point A and point B. As a result of this process, the brain of London taxi drivers is structured differently to most other people's: the area of the brain that concentrates on mapping is highly developed and larger than normal.

Neuroscience and learning

The Royal Society committee attempted to sum up the current state of the field in terms of the relationship between neuroscience and education, claiming that:

> Neuroscience studies have begun to shed light on the mental processes involved in learning... we explore the extent to which these new scientific insights can inform our approach to education... The new field of 'educational neuroscience', sometimes called 'neuroeducation', investigates some of the basic processes involved in learning to become literate and numerate; but beyond this it also explores 'learning to learn', cognitive control and flexibility, motivation as well as social and emotional experience. With the effective engagement of all learners as well as teachers, parents and policymakers, the impact of this emerging discipline could be highly beneficial. (The Royal Society, 2011)

This is a bold promise and not simply a recognition of what has already been achieved, largely in this century, but a clarion call to expand this work and incorporate our emerging scientific knowledge into new ways of delivering learning for young people but also, significantly, for adults. No learning leader working anywhere in the world, for any kind of organization, should ignore this exhortation.

What the report sheds light on is the fact that learning 'seems the most broadly and consistently successful cognitive enhancer of all' (The Royal Society, 2011: 12). What that means, in effect, is that:

> education can build up an individual's cognitive reserve and resilience, that is, the adapted response to stressful and traumatic events in illness, including brain injury, mental disorder, and normal aging. Cognitive reserve and resilience can be built up at any point during life... Keeping the mind active slows cognitive decline and improves cognitive abilities in older adults. (p 12)

In addition, the report makes a play for the use of digital technologies in learning. The report concludes that they can 'support individual self-paced learning for people of all ages' (p 12).

The report is not a eulogy to neuroscience and education. It stresses the dangers and the challenges associated with this area of research. It is easy to draw conclusions from half-digested science to make overstated claims that certain software or exercises will have transformational impacts on users. Most of these claims are simply inaccurate. There is also the danger of making misleading grand claims: this is already happening in the popular press where the genetic differences of individual brains are being used to justify social inequality and downplay remedial actions. There has to be some caution in using specific research findings too generally, but nevertheless what has emerged so far is stimulating, interesting and applicable to practice in corporate learning.

The Maritz Institute produced a White Paper in May 2010 that focuses specifically on the neuroscience of learning and how it impacts on corporate education. Its overarching conclusion is that:

> We spend most of our time focused on the content we want people to know rather than how they will learn. As a result, we fail to engage them, fail to keep them engaged, and fail to help them transfer their knowledge into action. Deep, lasting learning that results in changed performance does not happen. (Hendel-Giller et al, 2010: 2)

The report describes the work of Zull, whose research in 2002 linked the Kolb learning cycle to the structure of the brain. His four stages of learning are reflected in the basic structure of the brain: gathering experiences through the sensory cortices; engaging in reflective observation (drawing on the temporal lobe); creating new concepts in the prefrontal cortex and then actively testing through our motor cortices. In other words, the learning cycle reflects the very structure of the brain. 'Zull suggests that the power and duration of learning is proportionate to how many regions of the brain are engaged. The completion of the entire cycle is required for true change in behaviour and performance' (Hendel-Giller *et al*, 2010: 3).

This has obvious implications for learning and development. Profound behaviour change requires reflection, the opportunity to put the learning into practice, and time for discussion and informal processing among colleagues and alone. That is not usual practice! There also has to be explicit time allowed for the transfer of information into knowledge and new meaning. This process is more complex than simple memory: 'expertise is not about increasing working memory capacity – it is about organizing information in the brain and increasing the size of chunks' (Hendel-Giller *et al*, 2010: 6). Isolated learning is far less effective in helping learners make meaningful connections, tapping into their experience either in or beyond work.

Science also demonstrates that we remember and act on information much better when it is coupled with emotion: emotional engagement helps us learn. From all of this information, the authors adduce six design principles for corporate learning:

1 Engage the entire learning cycle. Make time for reflection, creation and active testing as well as absorbing new information.

2 Make a connection with the learners' prior knowledge and experience.

3 Create opportunities for social engagement and interaction as part of the learning process.

4 Engage both feeling and thinking. Learning needs emotion as well as intellect.

5 Actively attend to attention – gaining, holding and focusing the learners' attention.

6 Engage a maximum number of senses – especially visual – when designing learning. (Hendel-Giller *et al*, 2010: 6)

Brain rules

John Medina, a developmental molecular biologist and research consultant at the University of Washington School of Medicine and Director of the Brain Center for Applied Learning Research at Seattle Pacific University, has popularized contemporary neuroscience. His best known book is *Brain Rules*, which elaborates 12 principles taught by neuroscience. It is a self-help book designed to enable us to 'survive and thrive at work, home and school'; first published in 2008 it has gone on to sell hundreds of thousands of copies.

His 12 rules are worth elaborating as they define a context for building great learning environments for adults:

Rule 1: exercise boosts brainpower as it increases oxygen flow to the brain.

Rule 2: the human brain evolved. It is capable of highly complex thoughts and allows us to make decisions in a split second. It adapts to its environment.

Rule 3: every brain is wired differently and what makes the difference is both genetic and experiential.

Rule 4: we don't pay attention to boring things. Emotion matters.

Rule 5: we need to repeat to remember.

Rule 6: if we want to consign information to our long-term memory, we have to remember to reflect.

Rule 7: if we sleep well, we will think better.

Rule 8: stressed brains do not learn in the same way as unstressed ones.

Rule 9: we need to stimulate more of the senses, because all our senses work together and multi-sensory learning means better remembering.

Rule 10: vision trumps all other senses.

Rule 11: male and female brains are different.

Rule 12: we are powerful and natural explorers, therefore stimulating and cultivating curiosity is really important.

Essentially Medina takes 12 areas of neuroscience that are scientifically robust, explains the science behind each area and then shows how that rule could be applied in different contexts. In going down this path he effectively debunks a number of brain myths. First is the 'Mozart effect', the theory that playing classical music to young children (even babies) somehow helps their brains develop better. Second is the idea of left brain/right brain personalities, and the third is the idea that you can make your children smarter by playing language tapes while they are still in the womb!

What has all this got to do with work and learning? Medina is provocative and assertive:

> If you wanted to create an education environment that was directly opposed to what the brain was good at doing, you probably would design something like a classroom. If you wanted to create a business environment that was directly opposed to what the brain was good at doing, you would probably

design something like the cubicle... We can grow new connections, strengthen existing connections, and even create new neurons, allowing all of us to be lifelong learners... The adult brain continues creating neurons within the regions normally involved in learning. These new neurons show the same plasticity as those of new-borns. The adult brain throughout life retains the ability to change its structure and function in response to experience. (Medina, 2008: 271)

In other words, we can directly apply his logic to change both the work and the learning environment to make them more effective and efficient. Much of the research pushes in exactly the same direction. We have to create the right environment for learning. It needs to be relaxing and unthreatening, but nevertheless challenging. We need to immerse the learner in the complex multimedia experience that engages him or her intellectually and emotionally. Finally, we need to allow space for the learner to process the information, make meaning from it and eventually own that meaning in such a way as to change behaviour permanently. Not enough learning that goes on in organizations meets these three criteria. There is really no excuse for this. Literature is freely available and points to the same conclusions, whichever source you choose.

CASE STUDY   Dr Celine Mullins

Dr Celine Mullins is a psychologist based in Dublin, with a doctorate from Trinity College. She set up a company called Adaptas to exploit and develop her insights into the human brain and psychology. Her focus is on helping organizations change, first and foremost by changing the behaviour of their employees. If they take ownership of the process of improving their working and learning environment, organizational change follows more logically than if you attempt to do this the other way round. She is one of only a handful of neuro-psychologists, so far, who have chosen to work in the corporate learning field applying their research discoveries to organizational development. Her ideas have, therefore, high resonance in this chapter.

Dr Mullins believes that the brain likes to learn new things, and that learning new things actually keeps the brain healthier. If you can alter people's aspirations in both their working and their private life, by encouraging individuals to be more motivated and ambitious you can improve their health and wellbeing at the same time. This is a simple but powerful lesson from neuropsychology that has huge ramifications for corporate learning. That process of dissemination of research into organizational L&D is a rich process that makes learning more effective and makes people happier. If you are more conscious of how you learn you will be able to create better, more open, more communicative and more effective organizations. In a more effective organization, the workforce has the best possible opportunity to succeed and this of course makes the organization better and more successful. Dr Mullins subscribes to the virtuous circle I described earlier that links personal growth with organizational success.

Her mode of operation follows logically from these conclusions. She believes that we cannot develop organizations without starting with the individuals who work in them. The key point to start with is raising their awareness of how they could be working more effectively and helping them question the way things are organized currently. Her means of doing this is to take people out of their comfort zone so as to see the world with fresh eyes. They need to focus on possibilities for the future and on their ability to turn the possible into the probable. If they are uncomfortable or unhappy in the present, they can achieve a whole new level of comfort by moving towards a different place. What holds us back, she believes, is inertia coupled with fear.

Dr Mullins asserts that, when it comes to change, many people are profoundly scared that they will fail and fear of failure prevents them moving forward. They are also afraid of making things worse rather than better by interfering with the status quo. Overcoming fear is a powerful challenge, but the stronger the fear, the higher the excitement once you have made those changes. What she advocates is a move away from traditional, competent and safe learning and development into an environment that is much more challenging and exciting. She does not want her learning to be ok – she wants it to be transformational. The lessons from neuroscience underpin her whole approach.

The logic of this is that organizations need to build firmly into their culture an appreciation of the value of learning: it should be embedded and permanent. Learning should not be turned on and off according to annual budget constraints. If learning is embedded, it is a core element of the organizational culture. If this is the case, increased sharing of knowledge naturally follows, and this in turn will lead to improved personal and business performance. The process will lead to better teams and increased teamwork, and ultimately more effective organizations. This thesis really puts learning at the heart of any organization: if it wants to remain successful and respond to the challenges that our volatile and uncertain environment throws up, then an engaged staff, willing to learn and adapt, is a critical component of that process.

As the amount of knowledge that is generated by organizations and in their external environment increases rapidly, it follows logically that it is important to leverage and share that knowledge. Efficient sharing of knowledge eases the impact of change and encourages staff to modify their behaviour in the light of an evolving environment. It is possible to build new and efficient communication pathways that operate globally, informally and from the bottom upwards. These are almost like the neural pathways of an organization, and the more those pathways are used, the stronger the links and the stronger the collective experience. The core issue is, however, that none of this works unless the individuals involved want to make it work. The place to begin is with individuals. In some sense, learning is the breakthrough device to create knowledge and share the opportunities and insights emerging from knowledge, and using all of this to build a better, more productive learning environment. When this is the case, it is possible to inaugurate a process that will ultimately minimize bad behaviour and maximize support.

The brain, according to Dr Mullins, is optimal in terms of size and functions, but the structures within the brain have much more capacity for growth than is acknowledged or utilized by most people. The brain develops by making more connections between the neurons in the brain. The issue is not more neurons (we have over 100 billion) but more connections. The more connections, the more agility, and the more self-development. This is the same logic as Barbara Arrowsmith-Young deployed. At a very fundamental level this impacts on who we are and what we do but, above all, it demonstrates that the vast majority of people have far more potential than they recognize, and certainly far more potential than their employers recognize. This is why most people at work feel that they do not give their best. They do not articulate this in neurological terms, but neuroscience helps explain not only the size of the problem but the power of the solution.

The reptilian part of the brain is the oldest part, and is still in control of many of our behaviours and decisions. Dr Mullins believes that people will get closer to reaching their potential if they allow the more recent parts of the brain to take more control. This process can be learnt and ultimately enables us to self-manage our brains. If we can do this, we can better manage ourselves and control more of the environment in which we find ourselves. This impacts on who we are and what we do and, if we are better at managing ourselves, we should be far better at communicating with and managing other people.

By taking control of our behaviours and decisions, we become clearer on why we do things and therefore more conscious of who we are and our impact on others. If this process is developed within an organization, it impacts, profoundly, on the quality of leadership and our experience of work. In some fundamental way the brain of the individual is linked to the 'brain' of the organization in which he or she is employed. In other words, it is impossible to change the culture of an organization without changing the behaviours of the people who work inside it. You cannot build a new culture with slogans; you can only do so by changing the individuals who reside within it and letting that new culture emerge as a result.

In the same way that clarity from the top executives in a company helps to achieve clarity throughout the organization, clarity in the brain at the high end allows the other parts of the brain to be more effective (and less controlling). This focus on achievement leads to increased happiness and to stability. If we understand our brains better we understand ourselves better. If we understand ourselves better we have more chance of modifying our behaviour and, by extension, modifying the behaviour of an entire organization.

At a fundamental level, this is about understanding consciousness and how that relates to the mechanics of the brain. Again this translates in organizational terms to the problems of growth and change, or adapting to an evolving external environment. This helps explain why some fail to adapt and wither and die as a consequence. This process also allows organizations to absorb increasing diversity as they grow, and take on board new staff with new perspectives and new ideas. In other words, it is the process that allows an organization to re-make and re-establish itself in an almost continuous process of renewal.

Organizational learning

It is clear from a significant body of research that traditional approaches to learning inside organizations are severely limited in terms of impact. Standing up and telling is known to be ineffective and is therefore increasingly obsolete. It needs to be replaced by doing and taking action. This in turn increases empowerment and allows staff to take action to deal with issues and problems at an individual or organization level outside the specific learning environment.

It is no surprise then, that Dr Mullins' approach is experiential. She likes to put people in situations where they can directly experience some of the issues that are under discussion in order to see what happens, and to learn how to take action. To do that, the individual needs to feel safe and able to trust the process. As this moves forwards, the learners become teachers, the teaching continues outside the programme, and the impact continues with no direct intervention.

This defines the key role of orchestrator and facilitator. Much learning can occur if we can build a safe space for these interactions to occur and, through constant repetition, allow behaviour to be modified. This is learning by doing, learning by experiencing, and learning from processes that are gradually internalized and absorbed by the individuals as behavioural norms. It is not a solo effort, so a vital part of the process is the sharing insights with others and establishing common values.

This is why simulation is a powerful tool. Dr Mullins has developed complex and accurate simulations to play out the process of movement from old and new behaviours. It can take weeks of detailed and iterative work to build two hours of simulation. However, once it is right, it can work in a powerful way on the participants. Even just observing the body language of colleagues as they go through the simulation can be a powerful and insightful learning process. The simulation accelerates learning and is very efficient, engaging and enjoyable. We know that the brain works better and learns more when people are having fun, and by creating tasks and characters in a recognizable environment, it is possible to build something that is both a high-impact learning environment and extremely engaging.

Conclusions

Emerging from this chapter is the critical role of knowledge sharing and community building. Just as they are increasingly acknowledged as a core part of learning, we can see them as a core part of any healthy organization. As information access broadens, a more level playing field is created for decisions to be taken. The problem is that many organizations operate in an antiquated way, where information is hoarded and rarely shared. If there is a shift towards equality of access to information, there will be a shift towards more open communication and increased innovation. Learning can unlock that process.

This is an important move towards learning actively with others while being emotionally engaged. As neuroscience reveals more and more about how human beings learn, the more this approach appears to be validated. If you make better learning, you make better individuals and better organizations.

More and more young people are coming into the workplace familiar with role-playing and serious games. This will affect their attitude to decision making. They respond less well to being told what to do and much better to being given some autonomy and being allowed to explore. Instead of waiting for this to filter naturally through an organization, it is possible to accelerate these changes for all staff by creating new modes of learning and new ways of organizing business.

There is an important by-product: people who enjoy life and continue to learn have longer and healthier lives than people who do not. It is also true that people whose lives are coherent in terms of mission and values are happier and more relaxed than people whose working life does not articulate with their personal values.

We need to be much better at designing experiential learning that allows the brain to respond consciously and unconsciously. Organizations need to work out the most effective processes for managing their own change, as they adapt to their environment. Within this process, learning and development is critical but it is not the only solution or the only way in.

It is possible to do this online but special care must be taken to build a virtual environment that is as accurate a representation of the physical world as possible. Furthermore, working online (as in face-to-face), you need to make learning a collective rather than a solitary process. This is the most effective learning. Wrapped around this is a bigger conundrum: how do you convince people that they can learn better and more effectively, and that learning is a key to survival for both individuals and organizations?

What are the lessons for the learning leader? There are 10 key ideas that the learning leader should take away from this discussion on neuroscience:

1 Get involved in the debate and try to understand at least some of the literature. You do not need to be a neuroscientist but you do need to understand the basic direction in which the research is travelling.

2 There is a direct correlation between individual happiness, workplace environment, the level of innovation and organizational performance. It is important that these factors are brought together by the learning leader and not isolated one from the other.

3 The most successful organizational learning is carried out in groups, or at least allows a learning environment where discussion and debate can occur. If you are developing resources they should be multimedia, engaging and exciting. Focusing on building motivation and excitement will allow the learner to fill in any missing bits of the learning. Learning that is dull and unengaging, however complete, will never be as successful.

4 There is no such thing as organizational development that does not involve people. The learning team has a critical role in making organizational development work and in building and defending organizational values and culture.

5 Organizations need to stimulate curiosity and promote engagement in the work process. As the workforce ages it is even more important to consciously develop engagement and curiosity. Much of this should be done in groups to be effective.

6 The learning leader has an essential role in helping build a knowledge-sharing process. Using technology will be ineffective unless the individuals want to share and see the value in doing so. This should be a critical by-product of all learning.

7 Learning is both product and process. Even in the most rudimentary and straightforward of learning programmes, there is a way of delivering that encourages the right kind of attitude and resilience and builds the right kind of workforce. There is also a way of delivering learning that does the exact opposite. The workplace learning leader needs to be clear about this and have consistent values and methods that reinforce the move towards engagement, innovation and productivity.

8 Nothing much can happen in a miserable working environment, while a great learning environment can help create a great working environment.

9 Learning in organizations does not occur in isolation: it is part of the culture and should be non-negotiable. If the learning leader does not argue consistently for this, it is doubtful if anyone else will.

10 We are at the beginning of a revolution: we know much more than we did but we still have a huge amount to learn about learning. The more we know, the more we realize its significance and centrality in building 21st century organizations full of engaged and happy employees who are productive and successful. There will never be a time when this message is irrelevant.

Note

1 https://royalsociety.org/policy/projects/people-planet/

The importance of technology for learning

Introduction

We have been promising that technology will solve the problems of learning for a long time. Probably the most enduring item of learning technology, which survived for well over 100 years, was the humble piece of chalk. This enabled a teacher to constantly renew the message on the blackboard, and created physical space to deploy ideas, exercises, keywords and drawings. Learning transmission to the student turned information on the blackboard into notes in a notebook or even earlier onto a miniature blackboard (a personal slate). For most people in their 40s and older the blackboard is still a remembered part of school or higher education and was almost the only technology available apart from the occasional radio broadcast or recording. It acted as a simple metaphor for progression: the higher the level of your learning, the larger the blackboard in the teaching room!

The arrival of any new technology, from the blackboard to the computer, has always been hailed as a precursor to the transformation of learning. We have heard for 50 or 60 years that such and such a development will lead to the demise of the role of the teacher as we know it, yet both teacher and classroom continue to flourish.

The whiteboard, the overhead projector, even the interactive whiteboard are simply extensions of that tried and trusted technology. Even the early experimentation with educational television was just a transposition of the teacher from the front of the classroom to a TV studio. That promise of a revolution in learning really never transpired. A teacher on a TV screen was, unsurprisingly, never as effective as a real teacher in the room.

It took the launch of the Open University in 1968 to offer a significant, radical and technology-driven alternative to conventional models of learning. The University was open to everyone, produced its own textbooks using instructional designers to make them as interactive and accessible as possible, and set a new standard for learning materials that was copied all over the world. The books were supplemented and supported by lectures delivered by academics through the medium of radio or television broadcast at strange hours of the night or early morning. Some courses had compulsory week-long summer schools, conventional tutorials located right across the United Kingdom, and assignments as well as final examinations.

What was radical about the OU was not its use of technology but its commitment to delivering degree-level programmes to anybody who wanted to access them. All of this was managed by a complex computer system, but the computing element was entirely invisible to the student – it simply managed the dispatch of the materials and the student record system. The OU was copied, not because of its innovative approach to learning, but rather for its conventional approach to learning, delivered in such a way that it could genuinely reach a mass market.

Eventually an OU degree began to carry equal weight and status to a degree from any other institution of higher education. From the day of its launch it became, and remained, the largest university in the United Kingdom and one of the largest in the world; the launch of a Business School in 1983 to deliver part-time MBAs and other executive education courses, created the largest UK business school. The OU now has over 2 million graduates, and its influence permeates every walk of life. Although many universities offer programmes of learning that do not require fixed attendance on campus, the OU still has a unique role, and still fills its virtual classrooms year on year.

The OU developed a model of learning that became known as 'open learning', allowing the learner to select the time and place and, to a certain extent, the pace of learning while the institution took care of standards, assessment and award delivery. This became a model that was extended into a number of analogues at vocational level such as the University for Industry and LearnDirect.

Another stream of technology-enhanced learning emerged in the United States during the 1970s and 1980s. Companies like the Control Data Corporation, based in Minneapolis, diversified away from selling mainframe computers to delivering learning on a computer console that was regulated and controlled by its servers located in learning centres all over the world. This was known as PLATO (Programmed Logic for Automatic Teaching

Operations). Without a teacher, competencies could be developed and learning enabled for a subscription fee to the providing organization, which offered the customers a combination of hardware, process, software and content in a single package and for a single payment. It offered content ranging from high school to university level and survived into the early 2000s. The aim was to deliver self-paced learning in a way that would allow learners to move to mastery at whatever pace suited them. Computers were infinitely patient or could match the learning demands of the fastest student. The teacher became a technician whose job was to enrol and manage the student group and keep track of progress. The learning was organized, structured and delivered by the computer. Developed once, the content could be used an infinite number of times, substantially reducing the unit cost of learning; that is why many of the providers of this early computer-based training focused on core skills in maths, English, science and technology (Sorlie and Essex, 1978).

A third technology stream emerged out of the decision to provide online learning: there was a need to keep track of enrolment and to track student performance, independently of the content. These two needs came together in a Learning Management Systems, or LMSs, a term first used to describe the management system for the PLATO K–12 learning system (Educause, 2003).

All three of these streams continue to the present day. E-learning has trans-planted PLATO's crude mainframe technology. Online synchronous learn-ing has transformed into webinars and massive open online courses (now known as MOOCs). A webinar is, after all, a synchronous seminar delivered online instead of in the classroom, often with no modification of the slides and using a traditional form of one-to-many learning, and a MOOC is a series of these presentations linked to reading materials and assessments. There are over 50 different kinds of LMSs that manage online learning provision in large companies. E-learning courses delivered to the individual with no intervention from any tutor or teacher exist in their hundreds of thousands, and many people's experience of learning technologies falls into one or other (or indeed both) of these models. There are very sophisticated variants, but the core functionality remains the same.

In spite of promises and predictions, computer technology did not funda-mentally alter learning, at least until now. What we are seeing currently is the first radical shift for a century, where the process of learning is being radically transformed using a range of new technologies that enable different models of learning and different learning processes. This change is underpinned by a series of new demands on individuals at work and in response to the need to manage volatility, complexity, uncertainty and ambiguity in not just the workplace but our society as a whole.

What's new?

There are five new shoots sprouting from the roots of learning in and through technology that are important and that the learning leader should be aware of. These are discussed below.

1. Simulation, gamification and virtual worlds

The first is simulation, gamification and virtual worlds. None of these related technologies are new, but improvements in hardware and software have allowed far more complex simulations to be built relatively cheaply, which can substitute for effective but extremely expensive real-world role-play.

As a case in point, the Irish company ETU (**www.etu.com**) has commercialized research that emerged out of Trinity College Dublin and built a simulation platform that allows the provider to manipulate the simulations in real time, modifying the simulation as the user progresses or to suit different users. Instead of hardwiring a simulation, which makes it expensive to build and very difficult to change, this product allows the end-user to vary the outcomes of the simulation and make an infinite number of changes even after a simulation has been built. This is in contrast to many of the expensive simulation systems that allow any number of changes before the final build but, once built, the software simulation stands alone and cannot be changed without expensive modification and reprogramming.

Gamification applies the simple logic of gaming to other more prosaic forms of learning. It offers incentives to the learner such as winning badges, building leader boards or taking part in challenges of one sort or another. This allows areas of learning not traditionally associated with a game to incorporate games elements. As an example, the company HT2 has developed a product called CURATR that gamifies the process of curation. It is designed to work with any learning programme and incentivizes the students to share items of interest or comment on posts and questions and thereby win points that unlock gates to allow progression to the next stage. An engaged learner is a more effective learner.

What this means is that within a learning programme, the learner activity and sharing is rewarded. Students are able to praise the actions of fellow students and help them gain acclamation and recognition. This turns what might be seen as a zero gain pursuit – sharing ideas and insights with others – into a process where the greater the participation the greater the reward. The aim is to passively change behaviour by encouraging learners to do things differently, in the case above, become more like curators, sharing and disseminating resources, and more open to participation with their fellow students.

The technique is exactly the same as the one used by wearable fitness devices such as Fitbits, or Nike Fuel Bands that encourage the user to eat better, and exercise more by offering badges and rewards for attaining different targets and by competing with fellow members of their community. The aim is to encourage the user to unconsciously increase his or her exercise regime and thereby modify behaviour permanently, increasing health and fitness.

2. Learning environments

The second area is the development of comprehensive learning environments to encourage community and support rather than just courses. These are places where learning content is shared but also places that encourage discussion, cooperation and both synchronous and asynchronous learning. For example, the OU's Future Learn is a MOOC platform that pays much more attention to building an entire learning ecosystem than some of the other MOOC platforms, which focus largely on delivery of content. This parallels the development of more complex and learner-centred synchronous learning delivery platforms, which have gone beyond PowerPoint over the internet into areas that allow breakout rooms, whiteboard areas, live chat and discussion on top of content delivery.

3. Learning 'apps'

The third development is small-scale learning 'apps'. These are 'one-shot' applications that allow users to build their own custom learning environment and follow their own learning interests, app by app. Rather like building with Lego bricks, users choose how to craft that environment and which parts of it to accentuate. Most of these apps will seamlessly replicate from laptop to phone to tablet. This enables learning to be originated in one location and continued seamlessly in many others. Jane Hart, the founder of the Centre for Learning Performance Technologies (C4LPT) maintains a list of the top 100 learning apps,[1] an indication of how rich and complex the area has become in a very short time.

4. Using big learning data

A fourth development concerns learning data. Some of this is big learning data that allows impact to be measured, and information gleaned on the performance and effectiveness of learning programmes (see Chapter 8 on big data). Some of the data generated, however, is focused on individuals' performance and they can collect summaries of their learning in a way that is independent of the organization that delivered it or the employer that paid for it. For example, Learning Locker (**www.learninglocker.net**) uses the Tin Can (or the experience) API to allow a user to build up an open source, portable learning record store which, once set up, automatically gathers and stores data on performance (**www.tincanapi.com**). TinCan describes this process as a:

> new specification for learning technology that makes it possible to collect data about the wide range of experiences a person has (online and offline). This API captures data in a consistent format about a person or group's activities from many technologies. Very different systems are able to securely communicate by capturing and sharing this stream of activities using Tin Can's simple vocabulary.

Once built, it can be taken from one organization to another, independent of employer or software. It is in essence a repository for storing and tracking learning data that can be used by the employer, but also allows the individual learner to take that data and use it in a completely different context; the data stays with the learner rather than the provider or employer. Figure 10.1 describes in schematic form how the Tin Can API works.

FIGURE 10.1   Rapid development tools

5. Rapid development tools

The fifth area concerns rapid development tools: software packages that allow individuals with little technical experience to develop learning resources that are interactive and multimedia. Some of these, like Articulate (**www.articulate.com**) allow the building of interactive, multiscreen e-learning material from pre-build templates, or to use PowerPoint presentations as the basis for developing e-learning material. This is unsophisticated, but offers a fast development environment and meets a significant need for high quality but cheap online learning materials.

There are others such as Camtasia (**http://www.techsmith.com/camtasia. html**) that are built around screen recording and the development of illustrated examples of software or systems alongside simulations using video and voice-over. Other packages like Raptivity (**www.raptivity.com**) offer templates for developing interactive exercises that can be 'dropped in' to learning resources. Raptivity's new product, 'Learning Arcs' allows the learning developer to link a range of interactions into a small nugget of learning that can be used on its own.

All of these products are designed to help organizations create fast online content that looks good and is effective and interactive. There is a hierarchy of material development. At the top is the custom-built material that is crafted from scratch and is high quality and expensive to develop. In the middle are the author programmes like Articulate that offer less flexibility but are cheap to buy and help rapid development of materials. At the bottom of the pyramid are loose connections of resources that encourage learner exploration and development. These can include PowerPoint slides, pdfs, website links, podcasts and YouTube videos. The resources are curated but not built into packages.

Each of these areas has a number of technologies related to them and a separate development pathway. They are certainly not mutually exclusive and form a portfolio of current developments that suggests the direction of the fundamental underpinning technologies related to learning.

CASE STUDY Ben Betts, HT2

For some expert input, I talked to the CEO of HT2, Ben Betts, to help me understand some of the complexities that shape the future direction of learning technology.

Dr Betts believes that, although learning technologies are acknowledged as important in corporate learning and are visible everywhere, they should have a greater presence and be seen as more significant than they are currently. This is clearly a marker for the future.

The main development track for his company at the moment is the personalization of learning technologies. The fact that this is only stuttering into life is not due to a lack of appropriate tools and applications, but because the providers of learning see the need to control the learning environment and monitor individual performance as more important. In a risk-averse environment, it is hard to 'let go' by letting people run their own show, in their own way, and making their own choices. For him, this process of personalization is the only way in which corporate learning can make the kind of impact on the organization that makes it an integral part of the core process of work.

The traditional model of control leads to an over-reliance on tracking and audit functions with a consequent lack of attention to the quality of the learning experience. In other words, the ability to audit and process learning data takes precedence over the quality of the user experience. This, almost by definition, holds back the development of learning. For Ben Betts, this is now becoming a critical differentiator between employers attempting to establish a learning organization and those that are content to offer a portfolio of learning programmes. There are many consequences of this differentiation, and a widening gap between the two approaches. This is not so much a different choice of technologies but a different frame of reference, and it is this that leads to different technological choices.

The difference actually defines the nature of the learning experience. Essentially, one type of company focuses on delivering information and demands almost a replay in its learning programmes. The key statistic is completion, and the model relies on check boxes and simple tests of recall. The other type of organization encourages discovery learning, experiential learning, and the integration of learning and work. These two approaches emerge from the two different philosophies.

New learning technologies allow far more opportunity to learn informally as well as mine data and share knowledge. In the world of social networking, there is a blurred line between sharing insight, work-related data and more frivolous information. It is possible to harness this and create a huge number of organically growing networks of communication that allow learning and knowledge sharing to become synonymous. If this is applied correctly, status should be accrued by those willing to share, or willing to comment on material and supplement material that others have shared. This, in turn, marks a subtle shift: the role of the learning team switches from focusing on content development, to encouraging a plethora of learning and developing the ability of all staff to learn. Learning becomes the critical issue, rather than the content.

What we see therefore is a fork in the road in terms of learning technology development and deployment. There are still large, expensive learning management systems that define and control (and therefore limit) the learning experience and act as a bottleneck through which all learning has to be deployed. These in turn engender technologies that allow good quality, interactive content to be developed that will run on these management systems. The alternative is smaller applications that are more open in form and structure and that link to each other and allow an almost infinite combination of uses depending on the needs, inclinations and experience of the learner. In the former, the learning system is built by the organization and deployed to the learner with little variation. In the latter, a range of learning systems are made available for the learner to define and develop according to preference and learning need. One is about control, the other is much more focused on enablement and facilitation.

There is a noticeable shift towards those organizations wanting to create experiential learning opportunities and away from those trying to provide more formal and controlled learning opportunities. Ben Betts would strongly argue that the informal and experiential model offers a richer and more engaged form of learning than can ever be provided by cloned content transmission.

Dr Betts is sure that learning technologies drive learning and constitute a significant investment. They are important, but they could be much more significant than they are currently. For this to happen, the mindset has to change, and the development, engagement with and the sharing of knowledge has to be more creative and more enabling. Ben believes that eventually this contrast in approach, philosophy and mindset will have a significant impact. It will become an important differentiator between organizations and their success. The learning choices will have significant ramifications. If we are developing what we mean by work and offering a different kind of work environment, this will require a new approach to learning. This in turn will need different delivery systems and different technologies to make it work.

CASE STUDY   Sam Burrough, online learning consultant

Sam Burrough made that transition described by Ben Betts, above. He shifted from an e-learning creator to a builder of sustainable learning experiences. He believes that learning technologies are important in the same enabling way that other technologies help people do their jobs.

He differentiates between the technologies that enable learning, which are ubiquitous, and those specific technologies deemed appropriate for learning that are lower quality in terms of ambition and application. For him the big, powerful learning management systems are a stumbling block to creativity and flexibility. The starting point is always people, not technologies. The key issue is what they need to do and how you can best facilitate that. His approach is to use small tools that can be flexible and user-centred and to design a great user experience that drives enthusiasm for the learning. This has pushed him away from structured materials development towards curating a range of resources that engage the user and building ways to gaining their attention and enthusiasm.

He sees the developments in health monitoring (Apple's iWatch will focus on passive monitoring of key health indicators) so that performance can be improved in incremental steps based on the data received as a potential model for learning. He believes apps monitoring work performance could one day be directing learners to small behaviour changes to make effectiveness at work a continuous goal, not a one-off event.

It is important, therefore, to focus on solving problems at work rather than bring in a portfolio of learning technologies. What counts is what works in specific circumstances, and the necessary tools can be taken from anywhere. You work out what is needed by being inside a community that shares ideas and solutions; he is an avid user of Twitter for just that reason.

He believes that consumer technologies are far in advance of learning technologies and can be adapted and adopted for learning. Skype, for example, was not created for learning but it can be a very useful component of a learning environment. Yammer (a Twitter-like technology that is designed for use inside organizations) can be used for learning conversations just as well as any others.

He is careful not to deploy technology blindly. He is a great believer in the power of a small-scale pilot or prototype alongside careful feedback from the user as a way of defining what might work. If you 'mash-up' different small technologies it is easy to unpick and reassemble. It is about what works for specific circumstances at specific times and as things change so should the technologies.

Sam's bet for the future is on predictive adaptive performance support tools that could begin to do the same for work-based learning as the medical apps are doing for health monitoring. Again it is adapting something designed for the consumer and making it work in business, which he sees as the way forward. He believes that people at work can solve their own development problems, with the right tools and the right feedback, and if that engenders a sense of empowerment and control and re-establishes a love for learning and insatiable curiosity, learning and work mesh together in a very productive way.

Burrough's view aligns exactly with the comments by Matthew McGregor, Senior Digital Advisor to Ed Milliband. 'People often wonder what the next big thing is – but its actually lots of small things we should be interested in.' (Quoted in Wired magazine, June 2014)

Trends in learning technology

Personalization of the learning process

As we begin to learn more about the brain and have a clearer view of the science of learning, we will have to change the nature of the learning experience to become more efficient and more effective. Learning will be more profoundly personalized and geared to the needs of the individual. In the same way that the complex algorithm that Facebook deploys allows every single homepage it generates to be unique for each user, it will be possible to use technology to massively individualize the learning experience so that no one pathway through the learning will be identical to any other. The only way to execute this is by offering learners the opportunity to engage with a range of technologies that embody different ways and different approaches to learning and allow them to build a unique learning environment that works best for them.

In this world of personalization and personal choice, what you choose to learn and the process you select to learn becomes irrelevant as the emphasis continues to switch to performance. You will be measured, not on the number of courses that you've completed, but on how your learning has enhanced your performance and made you a more effective player in your organization. No one will really care how you got there: the important thing is that you are effective and that the learning organization facilitated that process.

Let the learner choose the device and the location for learning

The vast majority of organizations have realized that trying to create a uniform technology experience for all staff in terms of hardware and software is counter-productive and stifles creativity. Not only is the desktop becoming more personalized, increasingly (through bring your own device schemes – BYODs) the hardware itself is becoming a personal choice. Far from being expensive, this had led to cost savings along with increases in productivity.[2]

The idea that one size fits all in terms of technology is increasingly absurd, when we now have the wherewithal to deliver one size fits one. So what works for the corporate laptop or desktop works even better for corporate learning. The two concepts operate in parallel and feed upon one another.

New interfaces will emerge that define the learning experience and the user experience. They will be highly user-centred and will sit on the front of an increasing range of learning apps that will be cheap to deploy. There is an enormous amount of effort being put into developing a range of learning apps. Just as the advent of the iPhone and the iPad platforms enabled hundreds of thousands of developers to build small, focused, functional apps to enrich their respective platforms, a subset of app developments will be targeted at learning.

Some of these will survive, many will not, but the speed and flexibility of the development environments means that a whole range of apps can move into particular elements of the learning environment and make it richer and more useful to the learner. These apps will not be able to survive as independent entities but will need to be bolted onto bigger frameworks and help build a complex and rich learning environment. As they emerge, they will kill off the giant LMSs. The learning management systems of the future will not be one large piece of software but a virtual construct held together by APIs and common data formats.

Almost everything will be stored in the cloud rather than in local IT systems and will be accessible from anywhere and on any device. Learning will be technology-enabled and available when, where and in what format the user chooses. This will enable learning to be started on a desktop at work, continued on a laptop and perhaps completed on a tablet or smartphone. There will be no ugly transition, as seamless movement from one device and from one process to another will increasingly become the norm.

Personal learning environments

If you build a personal learning environment, the ramifications are significant. Learning will be seen more as a process of continuous learning that the individual owns, rather than one-off, time-limited injections of knowledge that someone else demands. This will support and encourage innovation and organizational change. This in turn could mean that every part of the organization will have its own learning specialist. This distributed model could replace the L&D department where all the specialists are clustered together. Learning will therefore be embedded across and within functional teams.

Use of learning data

All of this is underpinned by the systematic collection and analysis of data. This data is not just about learning, but concerns the perception and performance of the organization both internally and externally. This fast stream of data will be tamed by data analysis tools and presented by data analysis experts. Learning data is merged into the organizational data stream and forms part of the reporting and analysis process.

The corporate roll-out of MOOCs

MOOCs will emerge as a separate technological strand: not just courses offered by universities to the general public but learning platforms that can be used by anyone to build learning events and learning programmes. They will offer opportunities for new providers to offer tailor-made solutions to their customers.

The existing portfolio of courses that are called MOOCs now runs into thousands. Not only are they available for individuals to enrol on, they are being picked up and curated by corporate learning teams and offered to staff. Some huge companies are reducing their commitment to delivering their own generic programmes and are instead encouraging staff to access and enrol in a range of MOOCs that are deemed useful and appropriate.

Using these technologies, staff with no formal background in learning will be able to engage with providers to offer quite sophisticated and tailor-made learning programmes that could include assessment, support and extension work. It is now possible to build a comprehensive learning programme by bolting together a range of MOOCs from different providers in different parts of the world to meet complex learning needs.

Challenges and opportunities for learning leaders

Learning leaders face a really exciting future as learning becomes more central and more critical to the success of the organization they work for, but it also means that they will have to deal with the increasing complexities of IT. The key to all this is, essentially, to liberate learning from behind the firewall and allow it to take place whenever and wherever the learner chooses. This will require sophisticated stakeholder management and an engagement at a senior level with the organization as a whole to negotiate the correct protocols and permissions.

Learning leaders will have to be both the learning expert and learning technology expert. The role will be to define what learning can contribute to the transformation of the organization; the method will be technology-rich.

The changing role of learning leaders

The way that learning practitioners will survive in this changing environment will be to participate actively in external networks and share insights within their organization. In some ways this model will become one of the ways that workplace learning will become embedded.

Sharing of insights will become a valuable form of learning, as expertise is churned and freely shared. Both internal and external networks will grow, meaning that the difference between working inside the organization and working with external networks will blur, and the allocation of time to allow someone to become a member of a community of experts will be seen as part of the core role rather than something peripheral and marginal.

Keeping track of developments

As the technology market fragments, and the learning team needs to keep track of a large number of emerging and existing technologies, insight and knowledge to make the right decision about what to adopt will not emerge simply from within the learning team; it will require a wider consensus. Ultimately, learning leaders will define what works in their context, based on a deep knowledge of learning and technology as well as of the organization in which they operate. This, however, will be mediated by an external network, and an understanding of what is going on in other organizations, not just locally but globally.

If you look at a learning technology innovation such as BT's 'Dare to Share' – an initiative that encouraged staff in the organization to post notes and videos to highlight their expertise and insights – it is useful to reflect on the reason why this programme is still being quoted 10 years after it was initiated. This is not because it was either technologically complex or innovative, but because it was the right solution then and continues to be now. It was not only about sharing learning: it helped deliver a broader cultural change message that the company was seeking. This is learning *at* work, learning *as* work, and learning *in* work. The net impact of Dare to Share is far greater than any number of initiatives that exploited a new technology without being grounded in the culture of the organization.

CASE STUDY   Modern poetry and MOOCs

Modern Poetry, or 'Mod Po' as it is affectionately known, is one of the better-known MOOCs. It is based on an undergraduate module and is delivered by the English department of one of the most prestigious, expensive and highly thought of universities in the world – the University of Pennsylvania, founded by Benjamin Franklin in 1746.

The programme is the brainchild of Professor Al Filreis, the Kelly Professor of English, and the Director of the Center for Programmes in Contemporary Writing at the University of Pennsylvania. It uses the Coursera platform. Coursera is a not-for-profit corporation developed by two faculty members at Stanford University. The platform was initially adopted by Stanford University, Princeton, the University of Michigan and the University of Pennsylvania for the first group of MOOCs in 2012. The most notable university in the United Kingdom to adopt the platform is the University of Edinburgh, whose Vice-Chancellor Sir Tim O'Shea sits on its advisory board.

Coursera has had over 6.5 million students take its programmes since its inception. The initial four partners have now been joined by 103 other prestigious institutions, taking the number of participating universities to 107. Recent research by the University of Edinburgh on its MOOCs draws some startling conclusions about the net impact and the benefits of delivering such open programmes to communities all round the world. The study of the experience of 300,000 MOOC students reveals a high level of student satisfaction and vindicates the university's decision to get involved.[3]

The Mod Po course follows the conventional 10-week structure (based on an academic term) and is divided into one new theme, poet or idea per week. Just like many other MOOCs, assessed work is optional, but should the student complete all of the assessments satisfactorily, he or she will be awarded a university certificate. The course is wildly popular: in its second iteration, which started in September 2013. It started with 37,000 enrolments and ended with over 40,000 enrolments. It diverges from many of its contemporary cousins on either the Coursera or other MOOC platforms in that it retained the vast majority of participants for the entire programme. The programme has been extremely successful, and drawn attention around the world for its innovative approach to delivering massive online learning. It has a number of specific attributes that directly contributed to its success and that form an almost generic checklist of the effective use of learning technologies on this scale.

Professor Filreis has created a significant learning community rather than an enormous number of individual isolated students. He runs the programme in a specific physical location, the Kelly Writers' House, which is an old cottage in the middle of the university campus. By giving the programme a physical location, he can invite any students based locally to attend his weekly live expositions. He also does not deliver 'lectures'; rather he organizes discussions between himself, a number of teaching assistants he employs to help him run the programme, the local audience and the wider community who can join by phone, chat or Twitter. Everything is monitored so that contributions from participants can be included regardless of the medium used.

When you participate in a live session, it feels like it is taking place in someone's living room. It is informal, casual yet authoritative and well-structured. It is like an extended book group discussion. The result is not only engaging, it generates a sense of belonging and creates a natural bond between Professor Filreis, his teaching assistants and his students. While the live programme is being transmitted there is usually a live Twitter stream, a chat session, as well as message boards. All of these spaces for comments are being constantly monitored by the teaching assistants so that interesting points that emerge can be brought into the discussion. From time to time Professor Filreis takes telephone calls from students live on air, to discuss aspects of the programme. He usually ensures that these calls are from students based a long way from Philadelphia, which adds to the drama and excitement of the events.

In addition to this once-weekly live session, there is a panoply of videos, audio and text resources that enrich the topic under discussion. These too have their message boards and chat sessions attached so that anyone can comment at any time. The teaching assistants monitor the discussion and add their own comments during the week. They also stipulate certain hours when they are 'on duty' and can be contacted directly. They will answer questions, and queries or respond to issues during that period. With nearly 40,000 participants, this is obviously limited, but it does mean that every day of the working week, at some point you can be in direct communication with one of the key players in the programme.

The assessments are all peer marked: it would be impossible to handle the assignments any other way. Random samples of peer-marked assignments are checked by the programme staff, and peer markers are encouraged to be fair and positive in their commentary. Most of the students who submit assignments, therefore, act as peer reviewers to others at the same time. Each assignment has a minimum of three peer reviews.

Due to the direct student input, the contribution of the 8 or 10 assistants, the willingness of the programme to 'go with the flow' and respond to suggestions for content, and to highlight exceptional contributions by students, the programme generates a genuine sense of belonging and excitement.

Students who are co-located have formed breakfast clubs or meet to discuss the content or gather to listen to the weekly synchronous broadcasts as a group. It is so popular that some students have taken the programme more than once; some have indicated that they will take it for a third time when it runs again at the end of 2014.

Unlike many MOOCs, which are characterized by a significant dropout rate as they progress, this programme keeps hold of its students. Some MOOCS retain as few as 5 per cent of the starting students. The numbers actually completing the course are small, with even fewer turning in the assignments and receiving certification. In Mod Po, student numbers increase as the programme moves through its 10-week trajectory, and significant numbers continue to the end. The number submitting assignments is far fewer but this is always billed as an optional extra rather than an integral part of the programme.

The course makes no effort to create a neat coherent user interface. The online site is a random collection of documents in many media. Any component can be studied in any order at any time, and the website remains live and accessible right the way through to the beginning of the next programme iteration. As more and more people pass through the programme, their trail, in the form of resources and comments, enriches the site so that the starting point for the next iteration is never the same as the starting point for the previous offering.

The next sequence of the programme in 2014 will include groups of students in other institutions taking the course along with their local professor. This puts it into unknown territory yet again.

This model of learning appears to offer a number of generic conclusions. These include the need to drive active participation, and the primacy of developing a student community. Plus, if you deliberately try to build student ownership you will be rewarded with increased loyalty and better participation.

MOOCs are stand-alone initiatives and run alongside more conventional courses in the same universities: Mod Po, for example, is a conventional undergraduate programme run once a year. But the distinction is blurring as some universities take other universities' MOOCs as part of their programmes and the MOOC experience changes how the programme is delivered on campus, enriching the experience. Students can also take the MOOC themselves for revision or to deepen their understanding and learning.

Corporate learning will explore and engage with MOOCs sooner rather than later. Some will produce their own content and license the platforms to run them; others will engage with the existing programmes and encourage their staff to participate. One organization in the United States, CorpU (**http://www.corpu.com/academy/education**) has built its own MOOC platform and recruits well-known academics to deliver courses which it videos professionally and edits. It then sells 'seats' on the programmes to corporate learning departments and uses teaching assistants to work with small groups of learners to ensure that it is a quality experience and that the learning is embedded. This is almost like an Open University model which is, ironically, where this chapter started.

What should the learning leader do?

Here are 10 tips for dealing with technology and staying on top of technological change and innovation:

1 It is impossible to manage this process on your own. If you have a team, allocate one person to each of the five development strands that I discussed earlier in this chapter and report back on, say, a quarterly basis. Ask yourself, what is new? What meets the needs that we already have? What should we be keeping an eye on in the future?

2 You need an external network of learning leaders to meet, debate and discuss what is going on. This is an informal network and should be a high-trust environment where you can share and support each other. The Learning and Performance Institute in

the United Kingdom has set up CLO Connect to do just that.
The Masie Centre in the United States has its long-established
Learning Consortium that networks learning leaders from
250 companies.

3 Gather together a few 'scouts' to help you – colleagues who will
be prepared to share with you any new technologies they think may
interest you. If you have enough scouts, say three or four, you will
manage to stay on top of developments and in touch with a very
fast moving environment.

4 Committing too early to a specific technology can be very costly;
not moving fast enough can be very inefficient. One way of
minimizing the risks is to constantly prototype or pilot potential
solutions. If you do that, you build a low-risk environment while at
the same time ensuring that what you are proposing to develop or
purchase will deliver what it is supposed to for you and your
organization. The evaluation of any prototype must include some
form of impact measurement, so you can look at what it will do
for the organization set against the true cost of ownership.

5 You can crowd source much of this process. You need to
understand what the people you are trying to provide for really
want, and what interests them, and where they find it hard to be
enthusiastic. If, for example, you offer staff the chance to try out
three new applications and to comment on which is the most useful,
simple to use and so on, you will always get a good response.
Nothing you do should be in isolation and everything should be
with the end user in mind.

6 Do not define an IT strategy in isolation from the wider
organizational strategy or in from your overall goals for learning.
IT, however tempting, should not be an end in itself, but a strict
means to an end. If there is no clear business benefit from moving
down a particular IT pathway, you should probably avoid it.
Equally, if you can do what you intend to do faster and more
cheaply by investing in IT, it is probably worth making that
investment.

7 Governance is critical here. Any framework that is developed
should be owned by the organization. The best way to do this is
to ensure that the organization is fully invested in your strategy.
Creating a governance model that includes senior members of

staff from outside your department or area will give you a much better chance of moving forward in concert with the rest of the organization. Any technology framework should be owned across the entire organization.

8 Leverage what already exists. Tools that are already used by the organization such as Yammer (which mimics Twitter for internal use only) can be developed for learning. Servers designed to store company materials could be used for storing learning assets. As much as possible, align what you do and what you use with the rest of the organization.

9 If you work in an organization that is big enough to have a Chief Information Officer, make friends with him or her. There is no point in going to war with people in IT, nor is there any point in setting up a separate IT operation. You should see the Chief Information Officer or Chief Technology Officer as a massive asset, not a block.

10 Move forward on more than one front. Sometimes it is important to have something custom-built, but for every one of those expensive investments, rapid development tools or assembling resources together can deliver much more for much less. If everything is high-end you will build to do a little. If everything is low-end you will not succeed in moving big initiatives forward. Your learning technology strategy should be multifaceted. Cover areas that will make the learner's life easier alongside areas that will make *your* life easier. Never forget the learner, and never forget the power of an excellent user interface and a world-class learning experience.

Notes

1 The 100 Tools for Learning 2013 is available from Jane Hart's website: http://c4lpt.co.uk/top100tools/guide/ The list changes by around 10 per cent every year as new apps appear and old ones become less popular.

2 *Forbes* magazine, for example, talks of 'surges in productivity' in response to BYOD initiatives; see http://www.forbes.com/sites/centurylink/2013/04/26/byod-employees-bring-their-own-efficiency-to-work/

3 MOOCs @ Edinburgh 2013 Report #1, https://www.era.lib.ed.ac.uk/bitstream/1842/6683/1/Edinburgh%20MOOCs%20Report%202013%20%231.pdf

REFERENCES

Chapter 1

Clark, T C (2012) *The Employee Engagement Mindset*, McGraw Hill, Maidenhead

Clow, J (2012) *The Work Revolution: Freedom and excellence for all*, Wiley, Chichester

Depree, M (1990) *Leadership is an Art*, Doubleday, New York

Duffy, F (2008) quoted in Hardy, G *et al*, Preface to *Working Beyond Walls: The government workplace as an agent of change*, Office of Government Commerce, Norwich

Gallup (2013) *State of the American Workplace: Employee engagement insights for US Business Leaders*, Gallup, Washington, DC

Guillen, M and Ontiveros, E (2012) *Global Turning Points*, Cambridge University Press, Cambridge

Hamel, G (2007) *The Future of Management*, Harvard Business School Press, Boston, MA

Hamel, G (2009) The hidden cost of overbearing bosses, Tower Perrins survey quote, *Labnotes*, London Business School, London

Heerwagen, J (2008) The psychosocial value of space, in The Whole Building Design Guide, 23/05/08 http://www.wbdg.org/resources/psychspace_value.php

Kaner, S (1998) *Facilitator's Guide to Participatory Decision Making*, Jossey-Bass, San Francisco, CA

Kotter, J (1996) *Leading Change*, Harvard Business Press, Boston, MA

Kotter, J (2012) Accelerate, *Harvard Business Review*, November

Levering, R (1988) *A Great Place to Work: What makes some employers good – and most so bad*, Random House, New York

Stewart, H (2011) *The Happy Manifesto*, Happy Company, London

Strategy Dynamics (2013) *The Global Trends Report 2013: Towards a distributed future*, Strategy Dynamics SA, Geneva

Whitty, Sir A (2013) *Encouraging a British Invention Revolution: Sir Andrew Whitty's review of universities and growth*, HMSO, Norwich

Chapter 2

Cairncross, F (2002) *The Company of the Future*, Profile Books, London

Catlette, B and Hadden, R (2012) *Contented Cows Still Give Better Milk*, Wiley, Chichester

Chade-Meng, T (2012) *Search Inside Yourself: Increase productivity, creativity and happiness*, Tan Collins Publishing, London

Clow, J (2012) *The Work Revolution: Freedom and excellence for all*, Wiley, Chichester

Edmans, A (2011) Does the stock market fully value intangibles? Employee satisfaction and equity prices, *Journal of Financial Economics*, **101** (3), pp 621–40

Goleman, G (1995) *Emotional Intelligence: Why it can matter more than IQ*, Bloomsbury, London

Hamel, G with Breen, B (2007) *The Future of Management*, Harvard University Press, Boston, MA, p 254

Kotter, J (1996) *Leading Change*, Harvard Business Publishing, Boston, MA

McKee, A, Boyatzis, R and Johnston, F (2008) *Becoming a Resonant Leader*, Harvard Business Press, Boston, MA

Rao, S S (2010) *Happiness at Work*, McGraw-Hill, Maidenhead

Seligman, M (1990) *Learned Optimism: How to change your mind and your life*, Vintage Books, New York

Seligman, M (2002) *Authentic Happiness: Using the new positive psychology to realize your potential for lasting fulfilment*, Simon and Schuster, New York

Stewart, T A (1996) *Intellectual Capital: The new wealth of organizations*, Nicolas Brealey, London, p *xi*

Chapter 4

Battelle, J (2005) The 70 per cent solution, *CNN Business 2.0 Magazine*, 1 December

Casebow, P and Ferguson, O (2010) *Good Practice Survey*, Good Practice, Edinburgh

Cross, J (2008) *Informal Learning*, Pfeiffer, San Francisco, CA

Jennings, C (2012) Social and workplace learning through the 70:20:10 lens, 702010forum.com

Kidd, J R (1971, 1973) *How Adults Learn*, Associated Press, New York

Lombardo, M M and Eichinger, R W (1996) *The Career Architect Development Planner*, Lominger, Minneapolis, MN, p iv

Tough, A (1971) *The Adult's Learning Projects*, OISE, Toronto

Chapter 5

Brinkerhoff, R O (2006) *Telling Training's Story: Evaluation made simple, credible and effective*, Berrett-Koehler, San Francisco, CA

Brinkerhoff, R O (2013) Presentation to Learning Technology Conference, London, January, https://www.timetag.tv/learningtechnologies/play/18184

Brinkerhoff, R O and Mooney, T (2008) *Courageous Training: Bold actions for business results*, Berrett-Koehler, San Francisco, CA

Fee, K and Rutherford, A (2012) *Total Value Add*, Airthrey Publishing, Edinburgh

Kirkpatrick, D L (1970) *Evaluation of Short-term Training*, Monograph No 3, College of Education, University of Oregon, Eugene, OR

Chapter 6

Bickford, A (2012) Connect thinking, www.connectthinking.com.au

Clark, R (1992) EPSS. Look before you leap: some cautions about applications of electronic performance support systems, *Performance and Instruction*, **31** (5), pp 22–5

Gery, G (1991) *Electronic Performance Support Systems*, Gery Association, PLACE

Mosher, R and Gottfredson, C (2011) *Innovative Performance Support*, McGraw-Hill, New York

Raybould, B (1990) Solving human performance problems with computers. A case study: building an electronic performance support system, *Performance Improvement*, **29** (10), pp 4–14

Chapter 7

Allen, M (2012) *Leaving ADDIE for SAM*, ASTD, Alexandria, VA

Gagné, R M (1965) *Conditions of Learning*, Holt, Rinehart and Winston, New York

Gagné, R M, Wager, W W, Golas, K C and Keller, J M (1974) *Principles of Instructional Design*, (5th edition 2004), Holt, Rinehart and Winston, New York

Masie, E (2013) Crowd learning design, in Learning 2013 blog: http://www.learning2013.com/blog/item/crowd.html

Rossett, A (2009) *First Things First: A handbook for performance analysis*, Pfeiffer, San Francisco, CA

Rossett, A and Schafer, L (2007) *Job Aids and Performance Support: Moving from knowledge in the classroom to knowledge everywhere*, Pfeiffer, San Francisco, CA

Rossett, A and Sheldon, K (2001) *Beyond the Podium: Delivering training and performance to a digital world*, Jossey-Bass/Pfeiffer, San Francisco, CA

Chapter 8

Birst (2012) *White Paper: The Big Data Opportunity*, Birst, Inc, San Francisco, CA

CIPD (2012) *CIPD Annual Survey*, CIPD, London

Deming, W E (1966) *Some Theory of Sampling*, 2nd edn, Dover Publications, New York

Deming, W E (1982) *Quality, Productivity and Competitive Position*, MIT Centre for Advanced Engineering, Boston, MA

Handy, C (1984) *The Future of Work*, Blackwell, Cambridge, MA

KnowledgeAdvisors, *Metrics that Matter*, www.knowledgeadvisors.com

McAfee, A and Brynjolfsson, E (2012) Big data: the management revolution, *Harvard Business Review*, October, pp 64–8

Norris, D M, Mason, J, Robson, R, Lefrere, P and Collier, G (2003) A revolution in knowledge sharing, *Educause Review*, September, pp 14–26

Raine, L and Wellman, B (2012) *The New Social Operating System*, MIT, Boston, MA

Rappaport, E (2013) Presentation at Happiness Manifesto Conference, Google HQ, London, April 24th

Siemens, G (2011) First International Conference on Learning Analytics and Knowledge, Banff, Alberta, 27 February to 1 March, https://tekri .athabascau.ca/analytics, p 34

Siemens, G (2013) Blog: ELearnSpace: Learning, networks, knowledge, technology, community

Siemens, G and Long, P (2011) Analytics in learning and education, *Educause Review*, September/October, pp 31–40

Chapter 9

Arrowsmith-Young, B (2012) *The Woman Who Changed Her Brain*, Square Peg, London

Beauchamp, G and Kennewell, S (2004) The influence of ICT on the interactivity of teaching, *Journal of Education and Information Technology*, **13** (4), pp 305–15

Blakemore, S-J and Frith, U (2001) The implications of recent developments in neuroscience for research on teaching and learning, *Research Intelligence No 75*, April; summary report published in STU Mentor, August 2003, p 8, available in Academia Edu: http://www.academia.edu/2726280/ The_implications_of_recent_developments_in_neuroscience_for_research_on_ teaching_and_learning

Caine, R G and Caine, N (1994) *Making Connections: Teaching and the human brain*, Addison-Wesley, Menlo Park, CA

Claxton, G (2014) Presentation at the Learning Technologies Conference (www.learningtechnologies.co.uk/speakers/guy-claxton)

Hebb, D O (1949) *The Organisation of Behaviour: A neuropsychological theory* (new edn, 2002), Psychology Press, London

Hendel-Giller, R *et al* (2010) The Neuroscience of Learning: New paradigms for corporate education, http://www.themaritzinstitute.com/Perspectives/~/media/ Files/MaritzInstitute/White-Papers/The-Neuroscience-of-Learning-The-Maritz- Institute.pdf

Howard-Jones, P (2010) *Introducing Neuroeducational Research: Neuroscience, education and the brain. From contexts to practice*, Routledge, London

Klein, R (1999) The Hebb legacy, *Canadian Journal of Experimental Psychology*, 53, 1

Kramer, J (2012) Kramer Lecture, University of California Television (UCTV) 'The aging but resilient brain: keeping neurons happy', 16 April

Medina, J (2008) *Brain Rules*, Pear Press, Seattle, WA

Merzenich, M (2009) TED Talk, April, Growing evidence of brain plasticity (www.ted.com)

Plaza, M, Gatignol, P, Leroy, M and Duffau, H (2009) Speaking without Broca's area after tumor resection, *Neurocase*, 15 (4), pp 294–310

The Royal Society (2011) *Neuroscience: Implications for education and lifelong learning*, The Royal Society, London

Chapter 10

Educause (2003) *Course Management Systems: Report of the Educause evolving technologies* Committee Meeting 20 October, https://net.educause.edu/ir/library/ pdf/DEC0302.pdf

Sorlie, W E and Essex, D L (1978) *Evaluation of a Three-year Health Sciences PLATO IV, Computer-based Education Project*, ED161424, University of Illinois, Chicago, IL

INDEX

Headings in *italics* denote a publication and locators in *italics* refer to material within a table or figure.

CPSIA information can be obtained
at www.ICGtesting.com
Printed in the USA
LVHW041730150120
643722LV00006B/187